First World War
and Army of Occupation
War Diary
France, Belgium and Germany

24 DIVISION
73 Infantry Brigade
Prince of Wales's Leinster Regiment (Royal Canadians)
2nd Battalion
1 November 1915 - 31 January 1918

WO95/2218/1

The Naval & Military Press Ltd
www.nmarchive.com
Published in association with The National Archives

Published by

The Naval & Military Press Ltd

Unit 10 Ridgewood Industrial Park,

Uckfield, East Sussex,

TN22 5QE England

Tel: +44 (0) 1825 749494

www.naval-military-press.com

www.nmarchive.com

This diary has been reprinted in facsimile from the original. Any imperfections are inevitably reproduced and the quality may fall short of modern type and cartographic standards.

© Crown Copyright
Images reproduced by permission of The National Archives, London, England, 2015.

Contents

Document type	Place/Title	Date From	Date To
Heading	WO95/2218/1		
Heading	2nd Bn Leinster Regt 1915 Nov-Jan 1918		
Heading	2nd Bn Leinster Regt Nov-Dec 1915		
Heading	24th Division 2/Leicesters Nov 1915 Vol. XVI		
War Diary	Reninghelst	01/11/1915	02/11/1915
War Diary	St Eloi	03/11/1915	06/11/1915
War Diary	Reninghelst	07/11/1915	11/11/1915
War Diary	Voormezeele	12/11/1915	17/11/1915
War Diary	Reninghelst	18/11/1915	20/11/1915
War Diary	Eecke	21/11/1915	22/11/1915
War Diary	Arneke	23/11/1915	23/11/1915
War Diary	Watten	24/11/1915	25/11/1915
War Diary	Nordausques	26/11/1915	27/11/1915
War Diary	Ganspette	28/11/1915	30/11/1915
War Diary	Eecke	22/11/1915	22/11/1915
War Diary	Arneke	23/11/1915	23/11/1915
War Diary	Watten	24/11/1915	25/11/1915
War Diary	Nordausques	26/11/1915	27/11/1915
War Diary	Ganspette	28/11/1915	30/11/1915
Miscellaneous	2nd Leinsters	14/11/1915	14/11/1915
Miscellaneous	72nd Inf. Bde.	14/11/1915	14/11/1915
Operation(al) Order(s)	73rd. Infantry Brigade Operation Order No. 18	19/11/1915	19/11/1915
Miscellaneous	March Table		
Operation(al) Order(s)	73rd. Infantry Brigade Operation Order No. 19	21/11/1915	21/11/1915
Miscellaneous	March Table	21/11/1915	21/11/1915
Operation(al) Order(s)	73rd Infantry Brigade Operation Order No. 20	22/11/1915	22/11/1915
Miscellaneous	March Table		
Operation(al) Order(s)	73rd Infantry Brigade Operation Order No. 21	24/11/1915	24/11/1915
Miscellaneous	March Table		
Operation(al) Order(s)	73rd. Infantry Brigade Operation Order No. 22	26/11/1915	26/11/1915
Miscellaneous	March Table		
Heading	2/Leinster Rgt. Dec 1915 Vol. XVII		
War Diary	Ganspette	01/12/1915	31/12/1915
Miscellaneous	24th. Divl. No. G401	31/12/1915	31/12/1915
Miscellaneous	Officer Commanding	01/01/1916	01/01/1916
Heading	2nd Bn Leinster Regt Jan-Dec 1916		
Heading	2nd Battalion. Leinster Regiment. January 1916		
Heading	2 Leinster Regt Jan Vol XVIII		
War Diary	Ganspette	01/01/1916	07/01/1916
War Diary	Poperinghe	07/01/1916	14/01/1916
War Diary	Kruistraat	15/01/1916	15/01/1916
War Diary	Hooge	16/01/1916	19/01/1916
War Diary	Zillebeke Lake	20/01/1916	22/01/1916
War Diary	Hooge	23/01/1916	27/01/1916
War Diary	Zillebeke	28/01/1916	31/01/1916
Heading	2nd Battalion Leinster Regiment February 1916		
War Diary	Poperinghe	01/02/1916	07/02/1916
War Diary	Railway Wood	08/02/1916	13/02/1916
War Diary	Vlamertinghe	14/02/1916	14/02/1916
War Diary	Belgian Chateau	14/02/1916	14/02/1916

War Diary	Vlamertinghe	15/02/1916	17/02/1916
War Diary	Railway Wood	18/02/1916	20/02/1916
War Diary	Vlamertinghe	21/02/1916	24/02/1916
War Diary	Poperinghe	26/02/1916	29/02/1916
Miscellaneous	2 Leinster	08/02/1916	08/02/1916
Heading	2 Leinster Regt Feb Vol XIX		
Heading	2nd Battalion Leinster Regiment March 1916		
War Diary	Poperinghe	01/03/1916	03/03/1916
War Diary	Hooge	04/03/1916	08/03/1916
Heading	2 Leinster Regt Vol XX		
War Diary	Zillebeke	08/03/1916	12/03/1916
War Diary	Hooge	12/03/1916	15/03/1916
War Diary	Vlamertinghe	16/03/1916	19/03/1916
War Diary	Bailleul	20/03/1916	25/03/1916
War Diary	Red Lodge Ploegsteert	25/03/1916	25/03/1916
War Diary	Red Lodge	26/03/1916	30/03/1916
War Diary	Wulverghem	31/03/1916	31/03/1916
Miscellaneous	Casualties March 1916	02/04/1916	02/04/1916
Miscellaneous	24th Division		
Heading	2nd Battalion Leinster Regiment April 1916		
Heading	2 Leinster Regt Vol XXI		
Heading	Here with War Diary for April 1916		
War Diary	Wulverghem	01/04/1916	06/04/1916
War Diary	Kortepyp	06/04/1916	09/04/1916
War Diary	Wulverghem	12/04/1916	18/04/1916
War Diary	Red Lodge	18/04/1916	23/04/1916
War Diary	Wulverghem	24/04/1916	30/04/1916
Heading	2nd Battalion Leinster Regiment May 1916		
Miscellaneous	D.A.G. 3rd Echelon	12/07/1916	12/07/1916
Miscellaneous	Divisional Routine Order at 8th May 1916		
War Diary	Kortepyp	01/05/1916	06/05/1916
War Diary	Wulverghem	06/05/1916	12/05/1916
War Diary	Red Lodge	12/05/1916	18/05/1916
War Diary	Wulverghem	20/05/1916	26/05/1916
War Diary	Kortepyp	27/05/1916	29/05/1916
Heading	2nd Battalion Leinster Regiment June 1916		
War Diary	Kortepyp	01/06/1916	03/06/1916
War Diary	Wulverghem	03/06/1916	11/06/1916
War Diary	Red Lodge	12/06/1916	16/06/1916
War Diary	Locre	17/06/1916	19/06/1916
War Diary	Kemmel Shelters	20/06/1916	20/06/1916
War Diary	Wytschaete	20/06/1916	28/06/1916
War Diary	Wakefield Huts	28/06/1916	30/06/1916
Miscellaneous	2nd Leinster Regiment.	15/06/1916	15/06/1916
Operation(al) Order(s)	73rd. Infantry Brigade Operation Order No. 45	15/06/1916	15/06/1916
Miscellaneous	Relief Of The 73rd. Infantry Brigade By The 7th. Australian Brigade.		
Miscellaneous	Relief Of The 73rd. Infantry Brigade By The 7th. Australian Brigade.	15/06/1916	15/06/1916
Heading	2nd Battn. The Prince Of Wales's Leinster Regiment (Royal Canadians) July 1916		
War Diary	Locre	01/07/1916	03/07/1916
War Diary	Wytschaete Trenches	06/07/1916	08/07/1916
War Diary	Wytschaete	08/07/1916	08/07/1916
War Diary	Locre	09/07/1916	11/07/1916
War Diary	Bulford Cp	12/07/1916	19/07/1916

War Diary	Hugedoorn	20/07/1916	24/07/1916
War Diary	Saleux	25/07/1916	25/07/1916
War Diary	Molliens-Vidame	26/07/1916	30/07/1916
War Diary	Vaux	31/07/1916	31/07/1916
Heading	2nd Battalion Leinster Regiment. September 1916		
Heading	War Diary for month of September 1916 of 2nd Leinster Regiment		
War Diary	Longueval	01/09/1916	02/09/1916
War Diary	Mametz	03/09/1916	03/09/1916
War Diary	Fricourt Dernacourt	04/09/1916	05/09/1916
War Diary	Bruchamps	06/09/1916	18/09/1916
War Diary	Bruay	19/09/1916	22/09/1916
War Diary	Souchez	23/09/1916	30/09/1916
Heading	2nd Battalion Leinster Regiment. October 1916		
War Diary	Daly's	01/10/1916	09/10/1916
War Diary	Gouay Servins	10/10/1916	18/10/1916
War Diary	Berthonval	19/10/1916	26/10/1916
War Diary	Camblain L'Abbee	27/10/1916	27/10/1916
War Diary	Noeux-Les-Mines	28/10/1916	28/10/1916
War Diary	Maroc	29/10/1916	31/10/1916
Heading	2nd Battalion Leinster Regiment November 1916		
Heading	War Diary 2nd Leinster Regiment for the month of November 1916		
War Diary	Maroc	01/11/1916	30/11/1916
Heading	2nd Battalion Leinster Regiment December 1916		
Heading	War Diary of IInd Leinster Regt for month of December 1916		
War Diary	Loos (Front Line)	01/12/1916	05/12/1916
War Diary	Loos (Les Brebis)	06/12/1916	11/12/1916
War Diary	Loos (Front Line)	12/12/1916	17/12/1916
War Diary	(Bgde Support)	18/12/1916	24/12/1916
War Diary	Loos (Front Line)	25/12/1916	29/12/1916
War Diary	Les Brebis	30/12/1916	31/12/1916
Heading	2nd Bn Leinster Regt Jany-Dec 1917		
Heading	War Diary of 2nd Leinster Regiment for the month of January 1917		
War Diary	Les Brebis	01/01/1917	04/01/1917
War Diary	Maroc	05/01/1917	21/01/1917
War Diary	Les Brebis	22/01/1917	24/01/1917
War Diary	Maroc	25/01/1917	31/01/1917
Miscellaneous	A Form. Messages And Signals.	20/01/1917	20/01/1917
Heading	2nd Battalion The Leinster Regiment War Diary for the month of February 1917		
War Diary	Maroc	01/02/1917	11/02/1917
War Diary	Roeux Les Mines	12/02/1917	12/02/1917
War Diary	Fouquereuil	13/02/1916	28/02/1916
Heading	War Diary for the month of March 1917 of 2nd Battalion The Leinster Regiment.		
War Diary	Fouquereuil	01/03/1917	01/03/1917
War Diary	Hallicourt	02/03/1917	03/03/1917
War Diary	Ablain St Nazaire	04/03/1917	04/03/1917
War Diary	Souchez	05/03/1917	11/03/1917
War Diary	Sains En Gohalle	12/03/1917	16/03/1917
War Diary	Souchez	17/03/1917	31/03/1917
Heading	2nd Battn. Leinster Regiment 73rd Infantry Brigade 24th Division April 1917		

Type	Description	Start	End
Heading	2nd Leinster Regiment for the month of April 1917		
War Diary	Souchez	31/03/1917	04/04/1917
War Diary	Fosse 10	05/04/1917	09/04/1917
War Diary	Souchez	10/04/1917	14/04/1917
War Diary	Fosse 10	15/04/1917	18/04/1917
War Diary	Houchin	19/04/1917	19/04/1917
War Diary	Auchel	20/04/1917	20/04/1917
War Diary	Laires	21/04/1917	26/04/1917
War Diary	Auchel	27/04/1917	27/04/1917
War Diary	Houchin	28/04/1917	30/04/1917
Miscellaneous	Narrative of Operations of 2nd Bn The Leinster Regiment		
Miscellaneous	Preliminary Instructions Memorandum No 1	06/04/1917	06/04/1917
Miscellaneous Diagram etc	Preliminary Instructions Memorandum No 2	07/04/1917	07/04/1917
Miscellaneous	Preliminary Instructions Memorandum No 3	07/04/1917	07/04/1917
Miscellaneous	2nd Bn The Leinster Regiment	09/04/1917	09/04/1917
Operation(al) Order(s)	Operation Order No. 3 by Lt Colonel A.D. Murphy M.C. Commanding 2nd Bn The Leinster Regt		
Miscellaneous	Appendix A		
Operation(al) Order(s)	Operation Order No. 3 by Lt Colonel A.D. Murphy M.C. Commanding 2nd Bn The Leinster Regt	05/04/1917	05/04/1917
Operation(al) Order(s)	Operation Order No. 4 by Lt Colonel A.D. Murphy M.C. Commanding 2nd Bn The Leinster Regt	11/04/1917	11/04/1917
Miscellaneous	Coy R. T. O Quartermaster	11/04/1917	11/04/1917
Miscellaneous	C Form (Original). Messages And Signals.	12/04/1917	12/04/1917
Operation(al) Order(s)	Operation Order No. 4 (a)	18/04/1917	18/04/1917
Operation(al) Order(s)	Operation Order No. 5 by Lt Colonel A.D. Murphy M.C. Comdg 2nd Bn The Leinster Regiment	18/04/1917	18/04/1917
Operation(al) Order(s)	Operation Order No. 6 by Lt Colonel A.D. Murphy M.C. Comdg 2nd Bn The Leinster Regiment	19/04/1917	19/04/1917
Operation(al) Order(s)	Operation Order No. 7 by Lt Colonel A.D. Murphy M.C. Comdg 2nd Bn The Leinster Regt	26/04/1917	26/04/1917
Miscellaneous	24th. Division.	12/04/1917	12/04/1917
Miscellaneous			
Miscellaneous	Special Order Of The Day by Major General J. C. Capper C.B. Commanding 24th Division.	19/04/1917	19/04/1917
Miscellaneous		17/04/1917	17/04/1917
Miscellaneous	24th Division.	16/04/1917	16/04/1917
Miscellaneous			
Miscellaneous		13/04/1917	13/04/1917
Heading	War Diary of 2nd Battalion The Leinster Regt for the month of May 1917		
War Diary	Houchin	01/05/1917	09/05/1917
War Diary	Bellerive	10/05/1917	10/05/1917
War Diary	Le Bas	11/05/1917	12/05/1917
War Diary	Steenvoorde	13/05/1917	14/05/1917
War Diary	Devonshire Camp Near Busseboom	15/05/1917	31/05/1917
Heading	2nd Bn Leinster Regiment for the month of June 1917		
War Diary	Devonshire Camp	01/06/1917	01/06/1917
War Diary	Steenvoorde	02/06/1917	05/06/1917
War Diary	Ottawa Camp Nr Ouderdom	06/06/1917	12/06/1917
War Diary	Micmac	13/06/1917	19/06/1917
War Diary	Dickebusch	20/06/1917	22/06/1917
War Diary	Nr Ouderdom	23/06/1917	25/06/1917
War Diary	Nr Vierstraat	26/06/1917	27/06/1917

War Diary	Micmac Camp	28/06/1917	28/06/1917
War Diary	Nr Ouderdom	29/06/1917	29/06/1917
War Diary	Affringues	30/06/1917	30/06/1917
Miscellaneous	Memorandum No. 1	01/06/1917	01/06/1917
Miscellaneous	2nd Battalion The Leinster Regiment. Circular Memorandum No. 2	05/06/1917	05/06/1917
Miscellaneous	Memorandum No 3	06/06/1917	06/06/1917
Operation(al) Order(s)	Operation Order No 15 by Lt Colonel A.D. Murphy M.C. Commanding 2nd Bn The Leinster Regt	05/06/1917	05/06/1917
Miscellaneous	Memorandum No 4	06/06/1917	06/06/1917
Heading	War Diary of 2nd Battalion Leinster Regiment for month of July 1917		
War Diary	Affringues	01/07/1917	08/07/1917
War Diary	Len Wast	09/07/1916	09/07/1916
War Diary	Affringues	10/07/1916	17/07/1916
War Diary	Renescure	18/07/1916	18/07/1916
War Diary	Hazebrouck	19/07/1916	19/07/1916
War Diary	St Sylvester Cappel	20/07/1916	20/07/1916
War Diary	32.a.2.2 Sheet 28 N.I.A. Central	21/07/1916	29/07/1916
War Diary	Canada Street Tunnels	30/07/1916	31/07/1916
Miscellaneous			
Miscellaneous	Instructions For Companies		
Operation(al) Order(s)	Operation Order No. 27 by Lieut Colonel A. Dimurphy D.S.O. M.C. Commanding 2nd Battalion The Leinster Regiment	26/07/1917	26/07/1917
Miscellaneous	Addenda to Operation Orders No. 27		
Miscellaneous	1st Position (Approaching 1st Objective)		
Diagram etc	2nd Position		
Diagram etc	2nd Objective		
Miscellaneous	Circular Memorandum No. 2		
Miscellaneous	Circular Memorandum No. 3	28/07/1917	28/07/1917
Operation(al) Order(s)	Operation Orders No. 28 by Lieut Colonel A.D. Murphy D.S.O. M.C. Commanding 2nd. Battalion The Leinster Regiment	29/07/1917	29/07/1917
Miscellaneous	Ref. Operation Orders No. 28 Para 4		
Operation(al) Order(s)	Operation Orders No. 29 by Lieut Colonel A.D. Murphy D.S.O. M.C. Commanding 2nd Battalion The Leinster Regiment	30/07/1917	30/07/1917
Miscellaneous	Narrative of Operations undertaken by 2nd Battalion The Leinster Regiment on the 31st July 1917		
Heading	2nd Battalion The Leinster Regiment for the month of August 1917		
War Diary	Shrewsbury Forest	01/08/1917	01/08/1917
War Diary	Dickebusch	02/08/1917	04/08/1917
War Diary	Camp	05/08/1917	10/08/1917
War Diary	Canada Tls	11/08/1917	13/08/1917
War Diary	Micmack Camp	14/08/1917	14/08/1917
War Diary	Camp A Mickmack	15/08/1917	19/08/1917
War Diary	Dickebush	20/08/1917	22/08/1917
War Diary	Canada Tunnels	23/08/1917	26/08/1917
War Diary	Micmac	27/08/1917	27/08/1917
War Diary	Camp A	28/08/1917	31/08/1917
Miscellaneous	2nd Battalion The Leinster Regiment.		
Heading	2nd Bn. Leinster Regiment for the month of September 1917		
War Diary	Dickebush	01/09/1917	02/09/1917

War Diary	Trenches	03/09/1917	03/09/1917
War Diary	Inverness Copse	03/09/1917	06/09/1917
War Diary	Camp A Micmac	07/09/1917	10/09/1917
War Diary	H Camp Dickebush	11/09/1917	12/09/1917
War Diary	Camp H Dickebush	13/09/1917	13/09/1917
War Diary	Hallebast Cross Roads Camp	13/09/1917	14/09/1917
War Diary	Westoutre	14/09/1917	14/09/1917
War Diary	Berquin Billet Area	15/09/1917	19/09/1917
War Diary	By Rail	20/09/1917	20/09/1917
War Diary	Barastre Camp	21/09/1917	23/09/1917
War Diary	Haut-Allaines Camp (C.29.B.5.8)	24/09/1917	24/09/1917
War Diary	Hancourt	25/09/1917	26/09/1917
War Diary	Line Detail Camp	26/09/1917	29/09/1917
War Diary	Line	30/09/1917	30/09/1917
War Diary	Detail Camp	30/09/1917	30/09/1917
Heading	2nd Battalion Leinster Regiment for the month of October 1917		
War Diary	Hargicourt	01/10/1917	03/10/1917
War Diary	Front Line	04/10/1917	08/10/1917
War Diary	Hargicourt	09/10/1917	14/10/1917
War Diary	Front Line	15/10/1917	20/10/1917
War Diary	Hervilly	21/10/1917	27/10/1917
War Diary	Front Line	28/10/1917	31/10/1917
Heading	2nd Battalion The Leinster Regiment for the month of November 1917		
War Diary	Front Line	01/11/1917	03/11/1917
War Diary	Templeux	04/11/1917	09/11/1917
War Diary	Hargicourt	09/11/1917	15/11/1917
War Diary	Hervilly	16/11/1917	21/11/1917
War Diary	Hargicourt	22/11/1917	27/11/1917
War Diary	Templeux	28/11/1917	30/11/1917
War Diary		20/11/1917	30/11/1917
Heading	2nd Battalion The Leinster Regiment for the month of December 1917		
War Diary	Templeux Quarries & L. 10.a	01/12/1917	04/12/1917
War Diary	Hargicourt	05/12/1917	10/12/1917
War Diary	Hervilly	11/12/1917	14/12/1917
War Diary	Hargicourt	15/12/1917	18/12/1917
War Diary	Templeux	20/12/1917	21/12/1917
War Diary	Montigny	22/12/1917	27/12/1917
War Diary	Leicester Lounge	28/12/1917	31/12/1917
Heading	2nd Battalion Leister Regiment for the month of January 1918		
War Diary	Leicester Lounge	01/01/1918	05/01/1918
War Diary	Vendelles	06/01/1918	09/01/1918
War Diary	Hancourt	10/01/1918	21/01/1918
War Diary	Lester Lounge	22/01/1918	30/01/1918
War Diary	Montigny Farm	31/01/1918	31/01/1918

300 95
22/8/

24TH DIVISION
73RD INFY BDE

2ND BN LEINSTER REGT
JAN 1916 - JAN 1918
1915 NOV

FROM 6 DIV 17 BDE

To 29 DIV 88

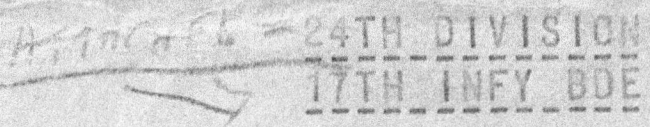
24TH DIVISION
17TH INFY BDE

2ND BN LEINSTER REGT
NOV - DEC 1915

73/94

24th Nararin

2/Leinster

Nov. 1915
Vol. XVI

121/7863

Army Form C. 2118

WAR DIARY
or
INTELLIGENCE SUMMARY
(Erase heading not required.)

Instructions regarding War Diaries and Intelligence Summaries are contained in F. S. Regs., Part II. and the Staff Manual respectively. Title Pages will be prepared in manuscript.

Place	Date 1915 Mar	Hour	Summary of Events and Information	Remarks and references to Appendices
ENINGHELST	1		Received orders to take over trenches north-east of ST ELOI from NORTH STAFFORDS to-morrow night instead of returning to our own "P" section.	
	2	10.30 am	Bn. staff reconnoitred trenches which are in a very bad state. Mud and water very deep and no dug-outs or shelters at all.	28th
			Pouring wet day	
		4.30 pm	Left camp and marched to VOORMEZEELE to take over new line of trenches. These were in a terrible state and communication trenches were in places two feet deep in mud and water. There are two lately exploded mine craters in front of the right of this line and there has been a considerable amount of bombing activity here lately. Bomb posts established on our edge of craters. Enemy have posts on opposite edges. Very wet night.	
ST ELOI	3	—	Still raining heavily. Trenches getting worse and therefore are falling in as fast as they are put up. Men working very hard but it is almost impossible to keep pace with the water	

Army Form C. 2118

WAR DIARY
or
INTELLIGENCE SUMMARY
(Erase heading not required.)

Instructions regarding War Diaries and Intelligence Summaries are contained in F. S. Regs., Part II. and the Staff Manual respectively. Title Pages will be prepared in manuscript.

Place	Date	Hour	Summary of Events and Information	Remarks and references to Appendices
ST ELOI	3	3.30 AM.	Enemy threw about 10 bombs at our posts at craters but this was checked by our rifle fire. Enemy's artillery fired about 15 rounds of light shell at our trenches without causing damage.	
"	4		Quiet day. Fine with some showers. All enemy is directed on the improvement of the trenches, and there is practically no firing on our front. The enemy is also in trouble with his trenches and can be observed pumping and baling.	
"		12.45 pm	A hostile aeroplane was engaged by one of our machines and brought down behind the British lines about two miles north of us.	
"		9 pm	Supposed running round craters. No bomb action.	
"	5		Quiet day. Our right company was shelled by whiz-bangs and suffered about eight casualties.	
"	6		Quiet. The state of our trenches has been much improved but they are still very bad. Owing to the inaction of the enemy — whose trenches	

Army Form C.2118

WAR DIARY
or
INTELLIGENCE SUMMARY
(Erase heading not required.)

Instructions regarding War Diaries and Intelligence Summaries are contained in F. S. Regs., Part II. and the Staff Manual respectively. Title Pages will be prepared in manuscript.

Place	Date	Hour	Summary of Events and Information	Remarks and references to Appendices
RENINGHELST	7		Company inspections, cleaning up and resting. Several men are suffering from bad feet after last trying period in trenches.	a.s.h.
"	8		Company training and instruction of grenadiers and machine gunners.	a.s.h.
"	9		Bn provided 150 men for R.E. working parties leaving camp on lorries at 9 A.M. and 150 men leaving at 8 A.M. Each party was away about 9 hours.	a.s.h.
"	10.	10 AM	G.O.C. 24th Division visited camp and transport lines.	a.s.h.
"	11	—	Wet day.	a.s.h.
POPERINGHE EZEELE	12	5.30 pm	Relieved 9/SUSSEX in P. sector. Very wet and trenches in very bad state. D Coy in reserve.	e.s.h.
"	13-14		Quiet days. Improvement of trenches is being continued but work is very difficult. Parapets and traverses are falling down in several places and the supply of R.E. material is very limited.	a.s.h.
"	14	12.30 pm	A patrol under 2/Lieut Brown made an exhaustive reconnaissance of our front, but met no hostile parties. Work was heard in progress in German trenches and a good deal of conversation	a.s.h.

1825 Wt. W593/826 1,000,000 4/15 J.B.C. & A. A.D.S.S./Forms/C-2118.

Army Form C. 2118

WAR DIARY
or
INTELLIGENCE SUMMARY.
(Erase heading not required.)

Instructions regarding War Diaries and Intelligence Summaries are contained in F. S. Regs., Part II and the Staff Manual respectively. Title pages will be prepared in manuscript.

Place	Date	Hour	Summary of Events and Information	Remarks and references to Appendices
	Nov. 15th.			
VOORMEZEELE	15		Received orders to exercise special vigilance to-night as a report of a probable attack has been received. Orders issued that nothing particular outside trenches are to be cancelled and that all men working in trenches are to be near their fire positions.	24th Bde letter G.457 attached
		5-8 p.m.	Our heavy artillery shelled the enemy's dumps, headquarters etc. in order to draw his fire. The enemy responded very slightly. Our field batteries cooperated. Transport with rations etc. delayed till midnight.	a.8.m.
		11.30 p.m.		
	16	-5.30 a.m.	Frequent patrols sent out but all report enemy quiet and nothing unusual observed.	
	15	8 p.m.	Our machine gun on night dispersed a hostile working party opposite Canadians. About 50 rounds were fired and there were shouts and sounds of confusion.	a.8.m.
	16	4-8.30 p.m.	Our machine guns traversed the road behind enemy's line and the point that appears to be this dump.	a.8.m.

Col. G. M. BULLEN-SMITH proceeded on leave

Army Form C. 2118

WAR DIARY
or
INTELLIGENCE SUMMARY.

(Erase heading not required.)

Instructions regarding War Diaries and Intelligence Summaries are contained in F. S. Regs., Part II. and the Staff Manual respectively. Title pages will be prepared in manuscript.

Place	Date	Hour	Summary of Events and Information	Remarks and references to Appendices
OORMEZEELE	Nov 17	1:30 AM	A German deserter belonging to the 148th Regt. 123rd Div., walked over and surrendered to our right coy. He was a very young soldier, intensely scared and clean. Sent him to B.H.Q.	
—	—	11:30 AM	Two "WHIZ-BANGS" near right coy's parapet. No casualties	a.a.h.
—	—	2 pm	Enemy fired several 5.9" H.E.un in area but did no harm.	
—	—	—	Two Germans shot this morning with telescopic rifles.	
—	—	8 pm	Relieved by 9/SUSSEX and returned to camp near RENINGHELST.	a.a.h.
RENINGHELST	18	—	Wet morning. Company inspections. Bomb instruction of N.C.O.s.	
—	—	5 pm	Officers attended lantern exhibition of aeroplane photos.	
—	19	—	Received orders for move of 24th Divn. to 2nd Army Rest area. The battalion will form part of a composite brigade starting tomorrow.	a.a.h.
—	20	4.30 AM	Bn. paraded and marched in brigade to EECKE via BOESCEPPE and GODEWAERSVELDE. Arrived at 10 pm. and billeted in town. Very cold night with hard frost.	O. Order No. 18 attached. a.a.h.
EECKE	21	—	Remained in village all day. Inspections etc.	
—	—	11 am.	Service for R.C.s in village church.	a.a.h.

Army Form C. 2118

WAR DIARY
or
INTELLIGENCE SUMMARY.
(Erase heading not required.)

Instructions regarding War Diaries and Intelligence Summaries are contained in F. S. Regs., Part II. and the Staff Manual respectively. Title pages will be prepared in manuscript.

Place	Date Nov.	Hour	Summary of Events and Information	Remarks and references to Appendices
EECKE	22	9.30 a.m.	Bn. left billets and marched in brigade to ARNEKE via CASSEL. One hour's halt for dinner 1 p.m. Arrived at 2.30 p.m. and billeted in farms north west of the town.	93 Bde. Op. Order No. 19 attached. a.8h.
ARNEKE	23	9 a.m.	Left billets and marched in brigade to new billets west of WATTEN. One hour's halt for dinner at 1 p.m. Arrived at 3.30 p.m.	93 Bde Op. Order No. 20 attached. a.9h.
WATTEN	24	—	Remained in billets all day. 2nd Lieuts DONN, GOUDIE, MORRISON, & CARLETON joined.	93 Bde. Op. Order No. 21 attached. a.9h.
—	25	9.30 a.m.	Marched in column with 13/MIDDLESEX to NORDAUSQUES and billeted in town. Arrived 11.30 a.m.	93 Bde Op. Order No. 21 attached a.9h.
NORDAUSQUES	26	—	Lt. Col. G.M. BULLEN-SMITH returned off leave and took over command.	
—	27	9.40 a.m.	Left billets & marched back to permanent billets west of WATTEN. Arrived about 11.30 a.m. Bn. billets are good but considerably scattered.	93 Bde op. Order No. 22 attached a.9h.
GANSPETTE	—	6 p.m.	Programme of work proposed for first 9 days training submitted to 93 M.B.	Copy attached.
—	28	—	Sunday. Services for R.C.'s	
—	29	9.30 a.m.	Commenced Platoon training. Hours of work — 9.30 – 8 a.m., 9 a.m. – 1 p.m. with occasional lectures and specialist parades in afternoon & evening. Received intimation that the 24th Divn. is in Army Reserve and must be ready to entrain at 9 hours notice.	a.9h. attached

2353 Wt. W2544/1454. 700,000 5/15 D.D.&L. A.D.S.S./Forms/C. 2118.

Army Form C. 2118

WAR DIARY
or
INTELLIGENCE SUMMARY.
(Erase heading not required.)

Place	Date	Hour	Summary of Events and Information	Remarks and references to Appendices
LANSPETTE	30/5		Training of platoons according to scheme submitted.	22nd

J.H. Walker
Lieut- Colonel
Comdg. 2/Hampster Regt.

Army Form C. 2118

WAR DIARY
or
INTELLIGENCE SUMMARY.
(Erase heading not required.)

Instructions regarding War Diaries and Intelligence Summaries are contained in F. S. Regs., Part II. and the Staff Manual respectively. Title pages will be prepared in manuscript.

Place	Date Nov.	Hour	Summary of Events and Information	Remarks and references to Appendices
EECKE	22	9.30am.	Bn. left billets and marched in brigade to ARNEKE via CASSEL. Bn. arrived at formups at 1pm. Arrived at 2.30pm and billeted in farms north-west of the town.	43 Bde Op. Order No. 19 attached. a.Bn.
ARNEKE	23	9am	Left billets for divisional formup. Arrived at new billets west of WATTEN. An hour's halt for dinners at 1pm. Arrived at 3.30pm.	43 Bde Op. Order No. 20 attached. a.Bn.
WATTEN	24	—	Remained in billets all day. 2nd Lieuts DUNN, GOUDIE, MORRISON, & CARLETON joined.	
—	25	9.30am.	Marched in column with 13/MIDDLESEX to NORDAUSQUES and billeted in town. Arrived 11.30 am.	43 Bde Op. Order No. 21 attached. a.Bn.
NORDAUSQUES	26	—	Lt-Col. G.M. BULLEN-SMITH returned off leave and took over command.	
"	27	9.40am	Left billets & marched back to permanent billets west of WATTEN. Arrived about 11.30 am. Bn. billets are good but considerably scattered.	43 Bde Op. Order No. 22 attached. a.Bn.
GANSPETTE	—	6pm	Programme of work proposed for first 9 days training submitted to 13 M.Q.	Copy attached.
"	28	—	Sunday. Services for R.C.s	
"	29	9.30am.	Commenced platoon training. Hours of work — 9.30 – 8 am. 9 am – 1pm. with occasional lectures and specialist parades in afternoons & evenings. Received intimation that the 24th Divn. is in Army Reserve and must be ready to entrain at 9 hours notice.	a.g.m. a.Bn.

Army Form C. 2118

WAR DIARY
or
INTELLIGENCE SUMMARY.
(Erase heading not required.)

Instructions regarding War Diaries and Intelligence Summaries are contained in F. S. Regs., Part II. and the Staff Manual respectively. Title pages will be prepared in manuscript.

Place	Date	Hour	Summary of Events and Information	Remarks and references to Appendices
GAMSPETTE	30.6		Training of platoons according to scheme submitted.	29a.

J.R. Nash(?)
Lieut- Colonel
Comdg. 2/Hampshire Regt.

SECRET.

> HEADQUARTERS
> 72nd INF. BRIGADE
> No. C.77
> Date 14.11.15

O.C.

2nd Leinster

COPY of
Herewith/24th Divisional Letter No.G.451,
dated 14.11.1915, for your information.

                                                Captain.,

Headquarters,   Brigade Major,
72nd Inf.Bde.,   72nd Infantry Brigade.
14.11.1915.

SECRET.

24th Division.
No.G.451.
14.11.1915.

72nd Inf.Bde.

In consequence of the enemy having shelled our roads and transport of caused some annoyance, the following action has been ordered by the V.Corps:-

(a). On the night of the 15/16th November, at 5.p.m. No. 2. Group, H.A.R., will shell the enemy's dumps, Headquarters, etc. in order to draw his fire.

(b). Should the enemy reply, the 17th Division will fire three red rockets from the neighbourhood of H.24.d.

(c). On the signal being given, ten rounds will be fired as rapidly as possible at a considerable number of points allotted to each of the Divisional Artillerys of the 9th, 17th and 24th Divisions. The Heavy Artillery will simultaneously fire at points outside the range of the Divisional Artillery.

(d). If the enemy continues to reply, a further five rounds per gun will be fired by all artillery under the instructions issued, (searching fire).

(e). Should the enemy continue to retaliate, fire will be turned on to the hostile batteries and continued until the enemy shelling ceases.

(f). The points and areas to be fired on are not in the enemy's front lines of trenches.

(g). The 24th Divisional Order No.25, dated 13.11.1915, regarding cessation of traffic in the forward area between the hours of 4 and 8 p.m., will not apply to the movements of Field Ambulance Wagons.

(h). It is possible the 2nd Canadian Division may participate in the firing.

Please acknowledge receipt.

(Sd). C.S.STEWART., Lieut.Colonel,
G.S. 24th Division.

Reference Sheets.
27 and 28. 1/40,000.
and 5a HAZEBROUCK.

COPY NO. 1

73rd. INFANTRY BRIGADE OPERATION ORDER NO. 18.

November 19th. 1915.

1.   The 3rd. Division will relieve the 24th. Division, which will be withdrawn into 2nd. Army Reserve.

2.   Headquarters, 73rd. Infantry Brigade, 5 Battalions (3rd. Rifle Brigade, 2nd. Leinster Regt., 9th. East Surrey Regt., 8th. Royal West Kent Regt., and 13th. Middlesex Regt.), 103rd. Field Coy. R.E., 73rd. Field Ambulance will march, as per attached march Table to billets about EECKE tomorrow, vacated by 76th. Brigade.

3.   All transport of Units will be formed up, in order of march of Units, facing South on the POPERINGHE-RENINGHELST Road by 2 p.m.. Head 500 yards N of cross roads in RENINGHELST, 50 yards distance between units. The Brigade Transport Officer will make all arrangements for the concentration.

4.   The 24th. Divisional Cyclist Coy. will picquet the road RENINGHELST-BOESCHEPE-GODWAERSVELDE-EECKE road during the march of the column and the O.C. Coy. will report for further instructions at 73rd. Brigade Headquarters at 10 a.m. on 20th.

5.   Arrangements for billeting will be notified later.

R Howlett

H.Q. 73 I.B.

19. 11. 15.

Major,
Bde. Major, 73rd. Infantry Brigade.

Copy No. 1. War Diary.
2. File.
3. 24th. Division.
4. 17 I.B.
5. 72 I.B.
6. 3rd. Rifle Brigade.
7. 2nd. Leinster Regt.
8. 8th. R.W. Kents.
9. 9th. E. Surreys.
10. 13th. Middlesex Regt.
11. 103rd. Fd. Coy. R.E.
12. 73rd. Fd. Amb.
13. 24th. Div. Cyclist Coy.

Transport at 1.15 pm along Poperinghe — Reninghelst road facing south. 50 yds interval between units

MARCH TABLE.

Order of march.	Starting Time.	Starting Point.	Route.	Remarks.
H.Q. 75 I.B.	4.45 p.m.	G.34.d.7.2.	Via BOESCHEPE-GODEWAERSVELDE-MECHE.	
Bde. Sig. Scet.	4.45 p.m.	G.34.d.7.2.		
3rd. Rifle Brigade.	4.45 p.m.	do.	do.	
8th. R.West Kents.	4.50 p.m.	do.	do.	
9th. East Surreys.	4.54 p.m.	do.	do.	
2nd. Leinster Regt.	4.58 p.m.	do.	do.	
13th. Middlesex Regt.	5.1 p.m.	do.	do.	
103rd. Field Coy.R.E.	5.5.p.m.	do.	do.	Will be halted short of road junction at G.34.d.10.7. at 5 p.m. to join the column.
75rd. Field Ambulance.	5.10 p.m.	do.	do.	

ISSUED AT 4 p.m.

Reference Sheet
27 HAZEBROUCK. 5A.
40. C.G.

COPY NO:- 8

73rd. INFANTRY BRIGADE OPERATION ORDER NO.19.

H.Q. 73 I.B. November 21st, 1915.

1.   The Brigade will march to-morrow to billets in area OCHTEZEELE - ARNEKE - RUBROUCK - BROXEELE - via ST.SYLVESTER - CAPPEL - CASSEL, as per march table attached.

2. **TRANSPORT.**
        All transport to march in rear of Units.

3. **BILLETING PARTIES, ETC.**
        Orders re billeting parties and arrangements for transport of blankets will be issued later.

R Howlett
Major,

ISSUED AT 1 p.m.   Bde. Major, 73rd. Infantry Brigade.

Copy No. 1. War Diary.
        2. File.
        3. Sig. Sect.
        4. 24th. Div.
        5. 13 M.X.
        6. 8 F.W.Kents.
        7. 3rd. R.B.
        8. 2 Leinsters.
        9. 9th. E.Surreys.
        10. 103 Fd.Coy.R.E.
        11. 73rd.Fd.Amb.
        12. 73rd. F.P.C.

MARCH TABLE.

ORDER OF MARCH.	STARTING POINT.	TIME.	REMARKS.
Bde. H.Q.	Cross Roads P.30.a.1.4.	10. a.m.	
Signal Section.		10. a.m.	
13th. Middlesex Regt.		10.1 a.m.	
8th. Royal West Kent Regt.		10.6 a.m.	
3rd. Rifle Brigade.		10.11 a.m.	
2nd. Leinster Regt.		10.16 a.m.	
9th. East Surrey Regt.		10.20 a.m.	
103rd. Field Coy. R.E.		10.24 a.m.	
73rd. Field Ambulance.		10.29 a.m.	

21/11/15.

Reference
Sheet 5A.
HAZEBROUCK.

COPY NO:-

73rd. Infantry Brigade Operation Order No.20.

H.Q. 73 I.B. November 22nd. 1915.

1.   The Brigade will march to billets tomorrow as per attached march table.

2. HALT.   There will be a halt for ½ hour at WATTEN where a meal should be provided for the men under Battalion arrangements.

3. TRANSPORT.   All transport except the blanket lorries will march in rear of Units. The blanket lorries will proceed direct to the new billets of units, commanders of which will give written instructions to the drivers.

4. BILLETING PARTIES.   One representative from each Unit will report at Bde. H.Q. at 8.30 a.m. tomorrow. Motor Cars will take them to the billeting area. Remainder of billeting parties will proceed on bicycles leaving the various H.Q. at 8 a.m.

It will be possible to arrange for the motor cars to make further journeys, C.O's may therefore detail one other representative to march with Bde. H.Q. from OCHTEZEELE at 9.15 a.m. and they will be sent forward in the motor to the new billets on return of the cars.

R. Howlett
Issued at 10.40 pm. Bde. Major, 73rd. Infantry Bde.

Copy No. 1. File.   No.10. 13th. M.X.
      2. War Diary.   11. 3rd. R. Bde.
      3. Sig. Sect.   12. BTO 73 I.B.
      4. 24 Div.   14. 73 F.P.O.
      5. 72 I.B.
      6. 2 Leinsters.
      7. 9 Surreys.
      8. 8 R.W. Kents.

MARCH TABLE.

UNIT.	STARTING POINT.	TIME.	ROUTE.	BILLET AT.
Bde. H.Q.	Cross Roads	11 a.m.	Via WATTEN.	EPERLECQUES.
Bde. Sig.Section.	½ mile S of the	11.4 a.m.	do.	do.
3rd. Rifle Brigade.	last E in	11.1 a.m.	do.	NORTLEULINGHEM.
8th/ Royal West Kents.	LEDERZEELE	11.6 a.m.	do.	BAYENGHEM.
9th. E.Surreys.		11.11 a.m.	do.	BAYENGHEM.
2nd. Leinsters.		11.16 a.m.	do.	EPERLECQUES.
13th. Middlesex.		11.20 a.m.	do.	GUEMY.
103rd. Fd.Coy. R.E.		11.25 a.m.	do.	EPERLECQUES.
73rd. Fd. Ambulance.		11.30 a.m.	do.	EPERLECQUES.
107th. A.S.C.		✻		

✻ Route to Starting Point via RUBROUCK and BROXEELE.

Reference sheet
5A HAZEBROUCK
1/10,000.

COPY NO:- 7

73rd. INFANTRY BRIGADE OPERATION ORDER NO.21.

H.Q. 73 I.B. November 24th, 1915.

1. The following moves will take place tomorrow, as per attached march table, in order that the 17th. and 72nd. Infantry Brigades will be able to halt for the nights 25/26 and 26/27 Nov. respectively in the 73rd. Bde. area.

2nd. Leinsters	to NORDAUSQUES.
13th. Middlesex	" ZOUAFQUES.
8th. R.W.Kents	" BONNINGUES (permanent billets)
3rd. Rifle Brigade.	" NORTEULINGHEM (" ")
9th. East Surreys.	" TOURNEHEM (" ")
103rd. Fd. Coy. R.E.	" MONTECOVE. (" ")

The two battalions of the 73rd. Infantry Brigade will return to 73rd. Brigade area on 27th. inst.

2. The O.C. 73rd. Field Ambulance will detail an ambulance to move in rear of columns 1 and 3.

3. Each battalion will detail two sections under an officer to march in rear of the Battalion to form up and bring in stragglers.

4. TRANSPORT.

All transport will march in rear of battalions.

5. BLANKETS.

All blankets must be collected at a central point for each battalion by 8.30 a.m. and a guard of 1 N.C.O. and 1 man left with them.

R Howlett

Major,
ISSUED AT 5.30 p.m.   Bde. Major, 73rd. Infantry Bde.

Copy No. 1. War Diary.   11. 13 M.X.
        2. File.   12. B.T.O. 73rd. I.B.
        3. Sig. Sect.   13. 73rd. Fd. Amb.
        4. 24th. Div.   14. 103 Coy. R.E.
        5. 17 Inf. Bde.   15. 73 Fd. Post Office.
        6. 72 I.B   16. Col. Oliver, 13 M.X.
        7. 2nd. Leinsters.   17. Lt.Col.H. de la Fontaine.
        8. 3 Rifle Bde.
        9. 9th. E.Surreys.
       10. 8 R.W.Kents.

MARCH TABLE.

UNITS ETC.	STARTING POINT.	TIME.	ROUTE.	REMARKS.
1 13th. Middlesex. 2nd. Leinsters.	Road junction ¼ mile S.W. of the E in EST MONT.	10 a.m. 10.5 a.m.	U in OUEST MONT- 1st. L in HELVELINGHEM -NORDAUSQUES.	Brevet Colonel L.G.Oliver will command the column from the starting point.
2 3rd. Rifle Brigade.				Not to reach road junction ¼ mile West of M in MONTECOVE before 10 a.m. & to be clear of it by 10.15 a.m.
3 6th. R.W.Kents. 9th. East Surreys. 103rd. Fd.Coy.R.E.	Cross roads ¾ mile S.W. of H in HOULLE.	10 a.m. 10.5 a.m. 10.10 a.m.	Main road NORDAUSQUES- St.OMER.	Lt.Col.H.de la Fontaine 9th. East Surrey Regt. will be in command of column from starting point.

Reference Sheet 5A.
HAZEBROUCK. 1/100,000.

COPY NO:- 5

73rd. Infantry Brigade Operation order No.22.

H.Q. 73 I.B. November 26th. 1915.

1. The 2nd. Leinster Regt., 13th. Middlesex Regt., and 73rd. Field Ambulance will move tomorrow, 27th. inst. to permanent billets as per attached march table.

2. The billets of the 2nd. Leinsters and 13th. Middlesex Regt. will be the same as occupied by them on nights 24th./25th. November, with a few modifications which have been explained to Battalion Billeting Officers.

The 73rd. Field Ambulance will billet at NOULIE.

3. All Transport will march in rear of units.

4. Transport for the blankets of battalion will be provided under Divl. Arrangements. Blankets must be collected at a central point in each battalion area by 9 a.m., and 1 N.C.O. and 1 man left in charge.

R Hoolett
Major,
Bde. Major, 73rd. Infantry Bde.

Issued at 5.15pm

Copy No. 1. War Diary.
2. File.
3. 24th. Div.
4. 24th. Div. "Q"
5. 2nd. Leinsters.
6. 13th. Middlesex.
7. 73rd. Fd. Amb.
8. B.T.O. 73 I.B.
9. 73rd. F.P.O.
10. Col. Oliver, 13 M.X.

MARCH TABLE.

UNIT.	STARTING POINT.	TIME.	ROUTE.	REMARKS.
2nd. Leinster Regt.	Junction of 5 roads ½ mile N of the second S in NORDAUSQUES.	10 a.m	First L in HELVELINGHEM. U in OUEST MONT.	Brevet Colonel L.G.Oliver, 13th.Middlesex Regiment, will command column from starting point.
13th. Middlesex Regt.		10.5 a.m		
73rd. Field Ambulance.			Via HELLEBROUCK.	To be clear of road junction 300 yards East of U in HELLEBROUCK by 11 a.m.

2/ Leinster Regt.
Dec 1915
vol XVII

24th Div.

Army Form C. 2118.

WAR DIARY
or
INTELLIGENCE SUMMARY.
(Erase heading not required.)

Instructions regarding War Diaries and Intelligence Summaries are contained in F. S. Regs., Part II. and the Staff Manual respectively. Title pages will be prepared in manuscript.

Place	Date 1915	Hour	Summary of Events and Information	Remarks and references to Appendices
LÀ GORGUE	Dec 1-16		Training carried on daily on a progressive system for about four hours daily. This included instruction of grenadiers, machine gunners, signallers and snipers. Platoon and Company training, route marches and lectures to officers and NCOs. Several officers and NCOs sent to school courses on grenade, machine gun work etc.	29th
	11	11:30 a.m.	The Army Commander inspected the Bde. on a route march and expressed himself very pleased with the marching and appearance of the men. Training continued under battalion arrangements.	29th 29th
	17	11:30 a.m.	Bn. carried out a practice attack on works specially made for instructional purposes.	29th 29th
	18	2:30 p.m.	The Regtl. transport of the Bn. was very favorably judged in four classes in Bde. competition for best turn out.	29th
	19	12 noon	A draft of 44 other ranks joined Bn. This is the first draft received since early August and brings the battalion strength up to about 640	29th

2353 Wt: W2544/1454 700,000 5/15 D. D. & L. A.D.S.S./Forms/C. 2118.

Army Form C. 211

WAR DIARY
or
INTELLIGENCE SUMMARY.
(Erase heading not required.)

Instructions regarding War Diaries and Intelligence Summaries are contained in F. S. Regs., Part II and the Staff Manual respectively. Title pages will be prepared in manuscript.

Place	Date	Hour	Summary of Events and Information	Remarks and references to Appendices
ANSPETTE	22	9-12 a.m.	Bn. route march with 1st line transport. Guiding march officers and scout officers inspected found trenches near MOULLE.	
"		4.40 a.m.	C.O., M.G.O. and four company officers left to reconnoitre new line of trenches north of YPRES which are now held by 49th Division and which will be taken over by the division next week.	
"		4 p.m.	Received preliminary orders for move of Divn. to new area by rail on 28th inst.	a.9.h.
"	23	11.30 a.m. 12 noon	Carried out second practice attack on German mental trenches. 2 drafts of 63 all ranks joined Bn. Strength now about 930.	a.9.h. 20.h.
"	24	6 p.m.	Officers returned from reconnaissance of new trenches.	
"	25		Christmas Day. Sports and contests in Regtl. Boxing Competition.	
"		1.30 p.m.	C.O. invited men at special dinners	
"		10 p.m.	Received news that move of Divn. was suspended until further notice.	a.9.h.
"	26	10 a.m.	Received news cancelling move of Divn.	a.9.h.
"	27	2 p.m.	C. in C. inspected part of brigade at training but did not visit battalion.	a.9.h.
"	28		Bn. training continued	a.9.h.
"	29			a.9.h.
"	30	7 a.m. 9 a.m.	Bn. route march. A demonstration by battalion grenadiers on clearing trenches day revealed German dead etc. at the mental trenches.	C.9.h.

WAR DIARY
or
INTELLIGENCE SUMMARY.

(Erase heading not required.)

Army Form C. 2118.

Place	Date	Hour	Summary of Events and Information	Remarks and references to Appendices
ANSTETTE	31	10.30 a.m	Inspection of the Bde. By G.O.C. 24th Division at HOULLE. Afternoon of coys, battalion marched past G.O.C. in column of route. Regimental transport also marched past.	Attached appendices "A" &c. ADM
			The following officers joined Bn during the month. On the 11th 2nd Lieuts W.P. LISTON, W.V. WHITBY, F.M. GAUNT, F.B. HUNTING. On the 13th, 2nd Lieut A.E. NYE. On the 5th, 2nd Lieut H.B. MOLLMANN, on the 6th, 2nd Lieut H.T. MOLL from 4th Bn.	AgM

G.H. Whitlock
Lieut Colonel
Comdg 2/4 Lancaster Regt

24th.Divl.No.G401.

Brigadier General
    Commanding 73rd.Infantry Brigade.

        On completion of my inspection of the Infantry Brigade Groups of the 24th.Division I desire to imform you that I was much pleased with the turn out, general bearing, and soldierly appearance of the troops.

        Though we all have still much to learn and cannot set our standard of excellence too high, I feel the utmost confidence in the discipline and moral of the division.

        We shall shortly again be engaged with the enemy - in a most important part of the line.

        I rely on all ranks in the division to do their utmost to defeat the enemy, recognising that hard work on all parts of our lines is necessary that we may get them in a better state to assist us in preparing for and bringing up troops for an attack, whilst enabling us to hold the lines with the minimum of troops; and endeavouring during our stay in the trenches in every way to increase our own moral superiority and lessen his by constant operations against him. So, when the time comes for serious offensive action, we will move forward with high heart in full confidence as to the reults.

        I congratulate you on holding the command of such a fine body of troops, and on the opportunities that you will possess, with their assistance, of doing good service for your King and Country.

31. 12. 15.   Signed. J. E. CAPPER,
                                          Major - General.

O'ROOM, 2 Leinster Regt.
No. 384
Date 1/1/16

HEADQUARTERS 73ʳᴰ BDE.
No. BM 9
Date 1.1.16

Officer Commanding,

2nd Leinster Regt.

   I have pleasure in forwarding the attached copy of a letter which I have received from G.O.C. 24th. Division, and I wish to express my gratification and pleasure to all ranks, and my appreciation of the good work done by C.O's, officers, N.C.O's and men, to earn the praise of the Divisional Commander.

H.Q. 73rd.I.B.
1. 1. 16.

        Brigadier General,
   Commanding 73rd. Infantry Brigade.

2nd Bn. Leinster Regt.

Jan - Dec. 1916

I

Jan '18

73rd Brigade.
24th Division.

2nd BATTALION.

LEINSTER REGIMENT.

January 1916.

2) Leinster Regt
Jan
Vol XVIII

Army Form C. 2118.

WAR DIARY
or
INTELLIGENCE SUMMARY.
(Erase heading not required.)

Instructions regarding War Diaries and Intelligence Summaries are contained in F.S. Regs., Part II. and the Staff Manual respectively. Title pages will be prepared in manuscript.

Place	Date	Hour	Summary of Events and Information	Remarks and references to Appendices
HANS PETTE	January 1915			
	1.	10.30 – 12.30	Sunday. C.O. Retrospection	A.D.K.
	3.	2 p.m.	Lieut Col MARINDIN, D.S.O. 19th Division lectured to officers at NORDAUSQUES on the new line to be taken over by the 24th Division	A.D.K.
	4.	9 a.m. – 1 p.m.	An advanced guard action against a flag enemy. Last day's training	A.D.K.
	5.	9 a.m. – 12 noon	Btn route march without transport	A.D.K.
	6.	7 a.m.	Advanced party under the Quartermaster left WATTEN station to take over new camp near POPERINGHE	
	7.	3.30 a.m. 5.30 a.m.	Transport left camp for AUDRICQ station. Bn. left billets and marched to AUDRICQ. Arrived 8.30 a.m. and had breakfasts from cookers near station. Started entrainment at 9.15 and train left at 10.15. Horses, wagons and ambulance party were shunted off at GODESWAERVELDE at 1 p.m. Bn. detrained just west of POPERINGHE at 2 p.m. Marched to camp in G.H.Q. (Sheet 28), 3 miles east of POPERINGHE	
POPERINGHE	8–13	2 p.m.	Found camp intensely muddy and in a very dirty and unfit state to camp in. General Reserve in rest camp. Officers and men confined to camp and all entertainments ordered to cease by divisional order.	

Army Form C. 2118

WAR DIARY
or
INTELLIGENCE SUMMARY
(Erase heading not required.)

Place	Date	Hour	Summary of Events and Information	Remarks and references to Appendices
POPERINGHE	11		1½ hours notice. Much clearing up of camp and transport lines to be done owing to specialists. All officers reconnoitred the Bn. area east of the YPRES canal.	28th
		3 pm	Captain W.S. CAULFEILD struck off the strength on appointment as staff Captain, 72nd Bde.	a.m.
	14	4.30 pm	C.O. and Coy commanders visited HOOGE trenches, returning at 3 a.m. 12th. Bn. moved to BELGIAN CHATEAU, south east of YPRES, moving by companies at 10 minute intervals. 3 Platoons of D Coy left behind in camp owing to shortage of accommodation at Chateau dugouts. Coy Bn. arrived at 6.15 pm. Bn. grenadiers and 4 Lewis machine guns with teams sent ahead to HOOGE trenches to relieve 1/North Staffords.	
KRUIGSTRAAT		11 pm	Sent 44 additional grenadiers to trenches to relieve North Staffords posts.	28th
	15	12 noon	The three platoons of D Coy left behind last night rejoined Bn.	
		5 pm	Bn. proceeded to trenches at HOOGE, relieving 1/North Staffords of 72nd Bde. 2 Platoons of D Coy for whom there was not accommodation in trenches were left at CHATEAU. All companies called at YPRES Asylum on their way to trenches and men exchanged their ankle boots

WAR DIARY
or
INTELLIGENCE SUMMARY

(Erase heading not required.)

Army Form C. 2118

Place	Date	Hour	Summary of Events and Information	Remarks and references to Appendices
HOOGE	16		for long wadero. Rifle bolts were soft at legs from I/C of storemen and labelled with men's name and platoon. Occupied trench outside of MENIN road, at HOOGE stables and road CRATER B and C Coys in front line, A Coy (3 Platoons) in support in rear of A Coy and 2 platoons of D Coy at H.Q. at HALFWAY HOUSE. 2nd Lieut F.B. HUNTING wounded in chest by sniper loose shelling of C3 and C4 (D Coy) and of OXFORD STREET.	A94u
		9 p.m.		
		10.30 p.m.	C Coy reported suspicious sounds which might be hostile mining in C5. Cleared trench for 30 yards and established wire cont posts.	Q8h
	17		Considerable shelling of C3 and C4 in morning. Slight damage. Guns guns retaliated. C Coy was enfiladed from south by enemy guns in afternoon. Casualties in C Coy:- 2 killed and 3 wounded by one shell. OXFORD STREET shelled by How'rs about 1/1 pm.	
		5-8 pm	D Coy relieved C Coy and A Coy relieved B Coy. One platoon of B Coy left in close support of A Coy in STABLES retrenchment. Rest returns to Bn H.Q before dawn. 2 Platoons of C Coy return to BELGIAN CHATEAU	Q8k

Place	Date	Hour	Summary of Events and Information	Remarks and references to Appendices
HOOGE	18	12:50am	Mining expert reports that explosions sounds in C.5. are caused by a family of rats. Trench again occupied	
"	19	1 am. 1 am.	Wet day. Top of the lungs and greater all through. Generation in nature of reliefs of 1/NORTHANTS. Enemy fired 20 shells round C.4.	a.9n.
"	"	11-12pm	" " " retreat to ZILLEBEKE dugouts Causing two casualties and slight damage	
"	"		Heavy artillery fire on our front caused enemy to relaliate severely on 14th Bde. trenches on our left.	
"	"	12:10 pm.	Received message from 14th Bde. "Please retaliate"	
"	"	7-9 pm.	Bn. relieved by 1/NORTHANTS and returned to ZILLEBEKE LAKE dugouts. 2 Platoons of C Coy. under 2nd Lieut LISTON form garrison of FORTINS 14 and 14 north of Lake. Ladders are exchanged for ankle boots at Asylum on the way back. Two Platoons of D Coy still remain at BELGIAN CHATEAU. Casualties during period 15-19 August. Killed: 3 ORs. Wounded. 1 officer, 10 ORs.	⊕ 9n
ZILLEBEKE LAKE	20-23		In Bde. support. Officers reconnoitre 2nd line positions which are to be held in case of attack. No movement in the open by day. Aircraft by day, and to give warning of gas by night. Working parties	⊕ 9n

WAR DIARY
or
INTELLIGENCE SUMMARY
(Erase heading not required.)

Army Form C. 2118

Place	Date	Hour	Summary of Events and Information	Remarks and references to Appendices
ZILLEBEKE LAKE	21.	4.30pm	of from 250 – 350 enemy night on HOOGE sector under R.E. Casualties during period 19–23 inst. – 4 wounded. 50 men of B Coy under Lieut Moll relieve garrison of 1H and 1K, also report their company at BELGIAN CHATEAU.	2B4.
"	22.	5pm	Lewis guns and trench relieve 4/NORTHANTS in HOOGE trenches	2.94.
" HOOGE	23.	6-8pm	Bn. relieved 4/NORTHANTS in HOOGE trenches. B and C Coys in front line. A Coy (less 1 platoon) in support, 2 platoons D Coy and 1 platoon A Coy in reserve at Bn. H.Q. Relief completed 10.15pm.	C94.
"	24	11.40am – 1pm	Whole battalion front heavily shelled by 4.5 and 5.9 Howrs and enfiladed by 77 m.m. Casualties – 3 killed, 11 wounded – and a good deal of damage to trenches caused. Our artillery retaliated and the Heavy Group also opened fire.	
"	"	10.10pm	Following message received from G.O.C. 24th Divn. "Warmly congratulate regiment on fine spirit displayed by all ranks under heavy strain."	
"	25	10 – 10.15pm	Enemy fired about 30 bombshell at C4 and C5. Two casualties and slight damage to trenches. Enemy fired about 30 lights shell in vicinity of MENIN ROAD barrier. No casualties.	2D4.

Army Form C. 2118

WAR DIARY
or
INTELLIGENCE SUMMARY
(Erase heading not required.)

Instructions regarding War Diaries and Intelligence Summaries are contained in F. S. Regs., Part II. and the Staff Manual respectively. Title Pages will be prepared in manuscript.

Place	Date	Hour	Summary of Events and Information	Remarks and references to Appendices
HOOGE	25	3.15	Enemy opened heavy bombardment with 5.9 H.E. on C.3, C.4, C.5, also on 92nd Bde line and between CULVERT and Y wood. Some shelling also on OXFORD STREET. No casualties. Our field guns and heavies retaliated.	AAA
"	"	4.30pm	G.O.C. 24th Division inspected trenches and went round front line.	
"	26		Enemy fairly quiet during the day.	AA13.
"	"	4pm	Ground in front of STABLES carefully patrolled by Lt Burn & Sgt- Leavey previous to a Bombing raid.	
"	27	12.30am	Two Bombing squads under Lt Burn & Sgt Leavey left our trenches & crawling close to the enemy lines heavily bombed his trench. Several grenades dropped into his trench & suddenly did considerable damage. Our Grenadiers returned safely without casualties & were supported by rifle fire at C.3 & Lewis Gun from C.5. Enemy quiet during the day. Battalion relieved by ye Northampto Regt; relief being completed by 11.0pm and proceeded to ZILLEBEKE LAKE dugouts and Jodunie L.H. & I.K. Reinforcement of 30 other ranks joined at Transport lines this day.	AAB

1875 Wt. W593/826 1,000,000 4/15 J.B.C. & A. A.D.S.S./Forms/C. 2118.

Army Form C. 2118.

WAR DIARY
or
INTELLIGENCE SUMMARY.
(Erase heading not required.)

Instructions regarding War Diaries and Intelligence Summaries are contained in F. S. Regs., Part II. and the Staff Manual respectively. Title pages will be prepared in manuscript.

Place	Date	Hour	Summary of Events and Information	Remarks and references to Appendices
ZILLEBEKE	28		Battalion in support; found working party by night; strength 550 men.	AA13
"	29	3 pm	"Gas alert" received from 9th 1.B. All precaution completed by 3.15 pm.	AA13
"	"	6 "	Working parties despatched totally 300 men.	AA13
"	30		Wind still being favourable to Enemy "Gas alert" still prevailed.	
"	"	6 pm	Working parties 300 men.	
"	31	--	"Gas alert" still on.	AA13
"	"	6 pm	Relieved by 1st Royal Fusiliers & proceeded to Camp C.	AA13
			Casualties period 28th – 31st Killed 1 Wounded 3 Accidentally Wounded 2.	
			The following drafts joined Bn. during the month 2nd 50 O.Rs. 2nd 55 O.Rs. 15th 37 O.Rs. 27th 30 O.Rs. total 173 other ranks.	--

J.H. Nicholson
H. Bol
Comdg 2nd Lincoln Regt

73rd Brigade.
24th Division.

2nd. BATTALION.

LEINSTER REGIMENT.

February 1916.

WAR DIARY or INTELLIGENCE SUMMARY

Army Form C. 2118

Place	Date 1916 FEB	Hour	Summary of Events and Information	Remarks and references to Appendices
POPERINGHE	1-5		Training of Coys carried on as per programme of work drawn up. Inspection of clothing, equipment and of men's feet.	A.9 hrs
"	6	2 pm	C.O. visited trenches to be occupied by Bn. in RAILWAY WOOD sector.	A.9 "
"	7	"	Coy commanders visited trenches as above.	
"	"	2.15 pm	Received wire from B.H.Q. ordering Bn. to stand to and report when ready to move with necessary transport.	4.O.C's requisition attached (A)
"	"	2.30 pm	Reported Bn. ready to move without transport.	
"	"	3.20 pm	Reported Bn. ready to move with all transport.	
RAILWAY WOOD	8	7 pm -11 pm	Relieved 8/WEST KENTS, 72nd Bde., in trenches of Divl. Line. 2.5 coys in trenches, 1.5 coys in YPRES ramparts. The 8th Div. is on our left, trenches are held very lightly and supports are provided. H.Q. in ramparts. Considerable hostile artillery activity particularly about MENIN road.	A.9 hrs
"	9	10 pm	Moved Bn. H.Q. to an advanced position in trenches. Moved two Platoons forward to support front line and relieved the garrison of support to one coy accordingly. Considerable shelling of roads and 2nd line trenches throughout the day but little damage was done. Wire cuts stated to Bn. 1/Com. 48 hours.	A.9 "

WAR DIARY
or
INTELLIGENCE SUMMARY
(Erase heading not required.)

Army Form C. 2118

Place	Date	Hour	Summary of Events and Information	Remarks and references to Appendices
RAILWAY WOOD	10.		Heavy enemy bombardment. A hostile patrol of an officer and six men were observed on for side of crater opposite A1. Bombs were thrown and the patrol dispersed. Considerable shelling of roads and vicinity of HQ & HELLFIRE Corner throughout the day and night. Two prisoners and seven men of A Coy wounded by shell at Pte RE dump. Cpl NOLAN killed	2.8ac
	11	4-10 pm	3 Coy relieved B Coy & A Coy relieved C Coy. C. Coy remain in supports. B Coy in reserve. Considerable shelling all day. H.20 and A1 were shelled about 11 am and the MENIN road and HELLFIRE corner again suffered. Bn H.Q. shelled with 4.2" Howr about 4 p.m. Sgt THOMPSON, Regt. Pioneer Sergt. wounded in YPRES and 2 stormer killed by shell.	
	12	4:10 pm	Enemy's artillery active all morning. About 4:10 pm what appeared to be a gas cloud was observed moving from our left across front of 6th DIV. A thin cloud passed across our front moving southwards. Gas helmets were donned in front-line and "Gas Alert" message sent. Heavy rifle and machine gun fire to our left. Ordered support and reserve coys to stand to. At 4.45 some bombs were thrown by enemy into crater near H.20 and a few enemy observed themselves on their parapet and were fired at.	
		6.30pm	"Gas Alert" cancelled as it has been ascertained that the cloud was a smoke barrage released by the enemy against the junction of 14th Div and 6th Div. Instructions received that no working or wiring parties are to leave trenches. Orders for our relief to night cancelled. Rations carried by 4/NORTHANTS and arrive 2.30 am.	R.8.Ac

WAR DIARY or **INTELLIGENCE SUMMARY**
(Erase heading not required.)

Army Form C. 2118

Instructions regarding War Diaries and Intelligence Summaries are contained in F. S. Regs., Part II. and the Staff Manual respectively. Title Pages will be prepared in manuscript.

Place	Date	Hour	Summary of Events and Information	Remarks and references to Appendices
RAILWAY WOOD	12.	8 p.m.	Bn. grenadiers who were relieved last night by 4/NORTHANTS returned to S.23. from rest huts.	
"	13		A very heavy bombardment of the HOOGE trenches occupied by 3/RIFLE BDE. commenced about 4 a.m. and continued almost without cessation until 5 p.m. All troops and dugouts while moved by enemy. Our artillery retaliation opened very soon and did not commence until the afternoon. Our front line was heavily shelled at intervals during morning and three casualties from trench mortars were incurred. During the early part of night HOOGE trenches were again heavily shelled at intervals.	
"		9 p.m – 2 a.m.	Bn. relieved by 4/NORTHANTS and returned to Camp E. between VLAMERTINGHE and OUDERDOM.	a.s.p.e.
VLAMERTINGHE	14		Cleaning up camp and inspecting of underclothes, clothing and feet.	
"		5.40 p.m.	Bn. ordered to Stand to. Bn. turned out and orders sent to transport.	
"		6.30 p.m.	Bn. ordered to move to BELGIAN CHATEAU. Adjutant sent to BHQ at YPRES for orders. Bn. left at 8.45 p.m. Necessary transport follows	

1875 Wt. W593/826 1,000,000 4/15 J.B.C. & A. A.D.S.S./Forms/C. 2118.

Army Form C. 2118

WAR DIARY
or
INTELLIGENCE SUMMARY
(Erase heading not required.)

Instructions regarding War Diaries and Intelligence Summaries are contained in F.S. Regs., Part II. and the Staff Manual respectively. Title Pages will be prepared in manuscript.

Place	Date	Hour	Summary of Events and Information	Remarks and references to Appendices
BELGIAN CHATEAU	14.		Bn. arrived about 8 p.m. and occupied dug-outs there.	
		10·30 p.m.	Orders received to return to camp. Cause of turn-out was the explosion of an enemy mine opposite H.13. Crater was occupied by 9/SUSSEX. S.O.S. signal sent. Bn. reached camp about 12.15 a.m.	A9A
VLAMERTINGHE	15.	—	Capt H.G. NEWPORT joined from hospital and 2/LT. L.D. BAILEY from 3rd Bn.	C9k
"	16.	8-11 p.m.	Working parties of 200 detailed from Bn. but cancelled at 10.30 p.m.	A9A
RAILWAY WOOD	18-20		Relieved 4/NORTHANTS at RAILWAY WOOD. Very quiet night and no casualties during relief. A quiet period in trenches. Comparatively little hostile artillery action, though WEST LANE and other trenches were slightly shelled each day. B and C Coys in front line.	
"	20	11.15 a.m.	"GAS ALERT" message received from Bde. and sent to all Coys. Wind N.E. LT. R.L. STIRLING reported from Hosp.	
		8-12 p.m.	Relieved by 4/NORTHANTS and Bn. returned to Camp E. Casualties during period 17-20 — 6 wounded.	A9A
VLAMERTINGHE	21		Lt. Col. BULLEN-SMITH proceeded on leave. Maj. ORPEN-PALMER in command. LT. H.C. BERNE joined Bn. Hard frost and very cold. Some snow.	A9A
"	22		Working parties of 200 detailed for trenches. Reported at 6 p.m. and 9 p.m., but first party unable to proceed owing to shelling of VLAMERTINGHE. Messages ordered 13th and 16th Bdes. H.q. 16th & Bde. of 6th Div.	C9k

Army Form C. 2118

WAR DIARY
or
INTELLIGENCE SUMMARY
(Erase heading not required.)

Instructions regarding War Diaries and Intelligence Summaries are contained in F.S. Regs., Part II. and the Staff Manual respectively. Title Pages will be prepared in manuscript.

Place	Date	Hour	Summary of Events and Information	Remarks and references to Appendices
LA MERTINGHE	23	10 am	Hard frost and snow in morning. Sent officer to POPERINGHE to take over billets for battalion.	
"	"	6pm–9pm	Working parties of 200 men conveyed to trenches in buses	
"	"		2/LT. B.E. McGUSTY, 3rd Bn. joined	
"	24	3pm	Bn. marched to POPERINGHE by coys at ten minutes interval. Billeted in Hop Factory near station.	2.9m.
POPERINGHE	26		Sent 400 men in two reliefs of 200 each for work on Canal line defences west of YPRES. Parties conveyed by train at 6 pm and 10 pm.	2.9m.
"	28	3.30 pm	Lecture to all officers and senior ncos. by O.C. 24 Div. on Discipline	2.8m.
"	29	3 pm	Company commanders inspected Decd. R.E. dump and examined stores available for same on indent.	
"	"	8.30pm	Received O.O. No. 28 ordering Bde. to be ready to move at one hour's notice after 12 noon tomorrow.	2.9m. O.O. No 28 attached

G.H. Waller Lt Col
Comdg 2/Monmouth Regt.

2 Leinsters

(A) The Brit Comdr has expressed his satisfaction with the report sent in on your turn-out at the "Stand to" yesterday

8/7/16

R Hoste? Major
Bm, 73 J B

HEADQUARTERS 73RD BDE.
No. AM 116
Date 8/7/16

XXIV   4/24

2 Leinster Regt
Feb
Vol XIX

73rd Brigade.
24th Division.

2nds BATTALION.

LEINSTER REGIMENT.

March 1916.

INTELLIGENCE SUMMARY

(Erase heading not required.)

Instructions regarding War Diaries and Intelligence Summaries are contained in F.S. Regs., Part II and the Staff Manual respectively. Title Pages will be prepared in manuscript.

Place	Date 1915 March	Hour	Summary of Events and Information	Remarks and references to Appendices
POPERINGHE	1		Battn held in state of readiness from 12 noon. Reserve rations received and issued to coys in billets. 36 boxes of SAA and Bn establishment of grenades brought up from transport and left at billets ready for distribution.	QMS
"	"	12.45 pm	Wired COMPLETE to BHQ.	
"	2	10.40 am	Orders for state of readiness cancelled.	
"	"	6 pm	Working party of 200 sent by train for work on 2nd line trenches behind HOOGE.	
"	"		Received Capt. Ordens re relief of North Staffords by battalion on night 4/5 inst.	CSgt.
"	3	2 a.m.	Lieut. Col. G.M. BULLEN-SMITH rejoined off leave.	
"	"	12.30 pm	Thunderstorm. Heavy rain all afternoon and rear station. Cleared afternoon and brought all men down to ground level.	
"	"	6 pm	Grenadiers and machine gunners left by train to take over from NORTH STAFFORDS in HOOGE trenches q/c. Coys went up to reconnoitre line.	QC him
HOOGE	4		Bn left POPERINGHE by train at 8.30 pm for YPRES nghm. Detrained there and after attaining numbers proceeded to HOOGE trenches in relief of 1/NORTH STAFFORDS. B and C Coys in front line, A Coy at Bn HQ and D Coy at BELGIAN CHATEAU.	QQR
"	4-8	—	A quiet tour in trenches. There was some bombing activity on the 5th but nothing	

1875 Wt. W593/826 1,000,000 4/15 J.B.C. & A. A.D.S.S./Forms/C. 2118.

XXIV 6/24

2 Leinster Regt
Vol XX

INTELLIGENCE SUMMARY

(Erase heading not required.)

Instructions regarding War Diaries and Intelligence Summaries are contained in F.S. Regs., Part II. and the Staff Manual respectively. Title Pages will be prepared in manuscript.

Place	Date	Hour	Summary of Events and Information	Remarks and references to Appendices
ZILLEBEKE	8		action was from two then moved, and there were no events of importance. Casualties during period :- Killed 5, Wounded 6. Very cold weather with snow	A.9.K.
"	8-12		Relieved by 4/NORTHANTS and returned to ZILLEBEKE BUND in support. Very cold with snow on ground. Working parties each night on HOOGE line.	C.9.K.
HOOGE.	12		Relieved 4/NORTHANTS in HOOGE trenches. Quiet night.	
"	13	3.30pm	A fine bright day. Enemy quiet in morning but about 3.30 p.m. he commenced a heavy bombardment of HOOGE and the trenches near MENIN road which lasted an hour. A great variety of shells used - chiefly 5.9" and 4.2" H.E. Our casualties 4 killed and 8 wounded. Our artillery retaliated effectively.	
"	"	10.45pm	Enemy shelled CULVERT and vicinity of GRAFTON street probably with a view to preventing work on repair of trenches damaged this afternoon. Our artillery again retaliated and silenced enemy about 12 midnight.	A.9.K.
"	"	10 pm	Sent a platoon of D Coy to relieve C Coy on STABLES retrenchment	
"	14		Quiet day. A Coy relieved B and D relieved C. C Coy to ZILLEBEKE BUND. Much good work done by night on strengthening front line and a considerable amount of new wiring erected. 2nd Lieut J.A. HOLMES joined from 4th Bn	A.9.K.

INTELLIGENCE SUMMARY

(Erase heading not required.)

Summaries are contained in F.S. Regs., Part II. and the Staff Manual respectively. Title Pages will be prepared in manuscript.

Place	Date	Hour	Summary of Events and Information	Remarks and references to Appendices
HOOGE	15.	2 pm	Enemy again bombarded HOOGE and trenches north of road with H.E. and shrapnel for one hour continuously. Our field and heavy artillery retaliated with effect. Our casualties – Killed 8. Wounded 10.	
"	"	9.30 pm	Relieved by 1/NORTH STAFFORDS and Bn. returned to Camp F. near VLAMERTINGHE. Last company marked out about 2.30 am	A9m.
"	"	~12 am	Draft of 134 other ranks who arrived at Transport Lines on 14th joined Bn. Casualties during period 12th – 15th Killed 19. Wounded 24.	
VLAMERTINGHE	16–19.		Battalion resting in Camp F. A working party of 100 men sent forward on G.H.Q. line on night of 16th. Fine weather and a comfortable camp.	A9m.
"	17.		St Patrick's Day. Scheme for R.Co. at 9.15 am and 12 noon in camp. Batts at POPERINGHE allotted to battalion in morning. A general entertainment for the battalion was arranged in the Bssl Cinema Hall and was kept up most of afternoon & evening.	A9m.
"	"	2.30 pm		
"	"	8 pm.	All officers serving with the battalion dined together in large room put for the first time since the beginning of the war.	
"	"	9 am.	Received Operation Order No 23 (72nd Bde), relating to move of brigade to new area near BAILLEUL on 18th and 19th inst.	Op. Order No 32 attached A9m

INTELLIGENCE SUMMARY

Summaries are contained in F.S. Regs., Part II. and the Staff Manual respectively. Title Pages will be prepared in manuscript.

(Erase heading not required.)

Place	Date	Hour	Summary of Events and Information	Remarks and references to Appendices
VLAMERTINGHE.	18		Received orders that Bn. would be ready to move to reserve any time after 12.30 p.m. as soon as relieving battalion arrived.	A.9.m.
"	19	12.30 pm	Bn. paraded and marched to new billets in Canadian Rest Area near BAILLEUL. Route via WESTOUTRE — MONT VIDAIGNE. Arrived new billets north of BAILLEUL about 4 p.m. Hot day.	A.9.m.
BAILLEUL	20-25		Training as per programme for 4½ hours daily. Officers visited KEMMEL defences and reconnoitred trenches to be occupied by battalion in case of emergency. Sent working parties to line at KEMMEL. On 23rd Coy officers visited new line to be occupied south of R. DOUVE.	
"	23		Lt-Col. G.H. BULLEN-SMITH took over temporary command of 43rd Bde. Major R.A.H. ORPEN-PALMER assumed command of Bn.	a.9.m.
"	25	2 pm	Bn. left billets and marched to new forward area via BAILLEUL and PETIT PONT. The C-in-C watched battalion pass through BAILLEUL and congratulated C.O. on the fine appearance of the men.	a.9.m.
RED LODGE, PLOEGSTEERT	—	5.30 pm	Arrived in huts and relieved 14th CANADIAN Bn. Bn in Bde reserve. Officers reconnoitred FLETCHER'S and CAVALRY trenches which will be occupied in the event of attack.	A.9.m.

Place	Date	Hour	Summary of Events and Information	Remarks and references to Appendices
RED LODGE	26		A/C Coys manned front-line and reconnoitred Bde. front. Lieut-Col. & M. BULLEN-SMYTH, D.S.O. reported Bn from BHQ	A9h
	27-30		2nd-Lt A.F. SMYTH joined Bn. Remained in huts. Improving camp, building dug-outs, and laying footboards. Working parties of from 200-350 men each night under R.E.	A9h
WULVERGHEM		8-9:30 pm	Relieved 4/NORTHANTS in right section of Bde line. A and C Coys in front line, B Coy in support and D in reserve. 2-Lt WHITBY slightly wounded and two men killed and five wounded by shell half-an-hour after relief.	A9h
	31		Quiet day with little shelling of our front. Casualties during month:— Officers, two wounded. Other ranks, 24 killed, 45 wounded. Total 71.	this statement should A9h

4/1/1916

J.M. Mitchell Lieut-Colonel
Comdg 2/Leinster Regt

No. 3mm 72
Date 74/16

CASUALTIES - MARCH, 1916.

UNIT.	OFFICERS			OTHER RANKS			TOTAL	REMARKS.
	KILLED	WOUNDED	MISSING	K	W	M		
1st R.FUSILIERS	-	-	-	6	10	-	16	
12th R.FUSILIERS	-	2/Lt.J.A.CAMPBELL	-	18	77	-	96	
8th BUFFS	-	2/Lt. W. DARLING	-	7	25	-	33	
3rd RIFLE BRIGADE	-	-	-	1	10	-	11	
8th JULKES	-	2/Lt. C.P.BURNLEY	-	3	22	-	26	
9th E. SUR.EYS	-	2/Lt.P.H.SCHOOLING ϕ 2/Lt.G.S.FETLEY + 2/Lt.T.H.YALDEN	-	8	34	-	45	ϕ died of wound + at duty
8th R.W.KENTS	-	2/Lt.N.L.GASCOYNE	-	2	17	-	20	
1st N.STAFFORDS	-	2/Lt.G.R.LOMAX	-	5	18	-	24	
9th R.SUSSEX	-	-	-	9	21	-	30	
7th NORTHANTS	-	2/Lt.J.E.GOODE	-	11	33	-	45	
13th MIDDLESEX	-	2/Lt.A.E.KING;Capt.K.WILKINSON 2/Lt. E.W.EVERS	-	10	41	-	54	+ at duty
2nd LEINSTERS	-	Capt. G.MURRAY + 2/Lt. W.J.WHITBY	-	21½	45	-	71	
12th R.G.Derbys.	-	-	-	2	16	-	18	
42nd M.G.COY.	-	-	-	-	1	-	1	
106th BDE. R.F.A.	-	-	-	1	4	-	5	
107th BDE. R.F.A.	-	-	-	-	1	-	1	
108th BDE. R.F.A.	-	-	-	-	4	-	4	
109th BDE. R.F.A.	-	-	-	-	-	-	-	
103rd FLD.COY. R.E.	1	Capt.A.IZAT 2/Lt.G.J.KINGSNORTH	1	-	3	-	5	
CARRIED FORWARD	1	14	1	107	382	-	505	

P.T.O.

24th DIVISION

CASUALTIES – MARCH 1916.

UNIT.	OFFICERS.			OTHER RANKS				REMARKS
	KILLED	WOUNDED	MISSING	K	W	M	TOTAL	
BROUGHT FORWARD	1	14	1	107	382	–	505	
104 FLD.COY.R.E.	–	–	–	–	3	–	3	
129 FLD.COY.R.E.	–	–	–	–	1	–	1	
17 I.Body.COY.	–	–	–	3	6	–	9	
GLASGOW YEOMY.	–	–	–	–	2	–	2	
72/1 T.M.BATTERY	–	–	–	–	1	–	1	
24V T.M.BATTERY	–	–	–	–	1	–	1	
TOTAL	1	14	1	110	396	–	522	

73rd Brigade.
24th Division.

2nd BATTALION

LEINSTER REGIMENT.

April 1916.

73rd Brigade.
24th Division.

2 Leinster Regt

Vol XXI

D.A.9.
3rd Echelon

Herewith War
Diary for April 1916

A.D. Murphy Capt &
                  Lt Colonel
6/5/16.   Comdg Leinster Regt

INTELLIGENCE SUMMARY

(Erase heading not required.)

Place	Date 1916 April	Hour	Summary of Events and Information	Remarks and references to Appendices
WULVERGHEM	1-6		Bn. in trenches in front of MESSINES. Line occupied is strong, front trenches sapped and well wired. Communication trenches bad but fair cover is obtained from the conformity of the ground and from hedges. On the 2nd and 3rd inst. the enemy bombarded the right company heavily causing some damage and slight casualties. Considerable shelling of supporting points and localities on these days also. Lieut. J.G. YOUNG wounded - shellshock. On the night of 3rd inst. B Coy relieved A, and D relieved C. On the 5th another heavy bombardment of whole section. Considerable damage in right company and several casualties in B & D coys. During this time boot looking parts on the right of Bn. section were advanced about 30 yards.	Q 8 u
"	4	-	A draft of 103 other ranks joined Bn.	a.s.r
"	5	11am	G.O.C. 24 Div. visited trenches	Q 9 u
"	6	8-9 pm	Bn. relieved by 4/NORTHANTS and returned to KORTEPYP	
KORTEPYP	-		NEUVE EGLISE Draft of 9 other ranks joined Bn. Casualties during period, 30 March - 6th April :- Killed - 6, Wounded 36.	Q 9 u a.s.r.

INTELLIGENCE SUMMARY

(Erase heading not required.)

Place	Date	Hour	Summary of Events and Information	Remarks and references to Appendices
KORTEPYP	6-12	—	Coys at training for 4½ hours daily. Working parties of 200 men employed on most nights at bringing cable near frontline. Weather fine but brighter.	asst.
"	9	—	2 /Lieut WHITBY rejoined from hospital (wounded)	asst.
WULVERGHEM	12	8 p.m.	Relieved 1/NORTHANTS in trenches. Quiet night. Received wire cancelling all leave and ordering all men on leave to be back by 18th inst.	asst.
"	12-18	—	A quieter time than last time. On the 13th FORT OSBORNE and BREWERS BUNGALOWS were heavily shelled and it was decided to evacuate the latter locality and to accommodate the people at BARBARY COAST. About 4 p.m. artillery reported a party of about 150 Germans moving east to west towards ONTARIO FARM. Later a number party were observed from our front line going in opposite direction. Our guns opened fire and timely dispersed what was apparently a daylight relief. On succeeding days, there was generally hostile artillery fire on or near our front line and behind from points that must mean shelling our alone.	

INTELLIGENCE SUMMARY

(Erase heading not required.)

Place	Date	Hour	Summary of Events and Information	Remarks and references to Appendices
WOLVERGHEM	12-18		Our front line is now held very lightly by day — two platoons being withdrawn from right coy and one platoon from left coy. on 14th. G.O.C. 24th Div. went round front line. On 15th, centre relief took place. Weather cold and the two last days wet and unpleasant. Casualties during period 12-18 — Killed 4, wounded 16. Total 20. Captain C.C. BARRY, 3rd Bn. joined.	A.9th
"	17	-		A.9th
"	18	11 am	Relieved by 7/NORTHANTS and returned to Bde reserve at RED LODGE	
RED LODGE	18-24		Bn. in Bde. reserve. Working parties of from 200-430 men each night. Weather cold with very heavy rain on 22nd.	A.9th
"	20	12 noon	R.G.C. inspected regimental transport of battalion and expressed his great pleasure at the excellent turn-out of horses, vehicles, and men.	A.9th
"	21		Maj. R. ORPEN-PALMER left Bn. to take temporary command of 2.13/MIDDLESEX Regt.	A.9th
"	"	4.20 pm	Received message from Bde. reporting that our artillery had exploded some gas cylinders in enemy's trenches on right of the 50th Div. on our left. Dense clouds of gas rose in the air. This occurred at 5.30 pm	
"	"	10.30 pm	Received "GAS ALERT" message	Q.9. &c

INTELLIGENCE SUMMARY

Instructions regarding War Diaries and Intelligence Summaries are contained in F.S. Regs., Part II. and the Staff Manual respectively. Title Pages will be prepared in manuscript.

(Erase heading not required.)

Place	Date	Hour	Summary of Events and Information	Remarks and references to Appendices
RED LODGE	22	11.30 p.m.	"GAS ALERT" cancelled. Very wet day.	A.9.h.
"	23	4 a.m.	Posted two control posts to prevent movement by daylight on HILL 63	A.9.h.
WULVERGHEM	24	11.30 p.m. – 1 a.m.	Relieved 1/NORTHAMPTONS in trenches.	
"	25		Enemy shelled C.J. trench with 5.9 Howitzer and H.E. shells.	A.a.B
"	"	8.30-12.30	Working parties on DIAGONAL, MOSLANE and KING EDWARD trenches	A.a.B
"	26	9 a.m.	Lt-Col Bullen Smith D.S.O. took command of 93rd Inf. Bde. Captain A.D. Murphy in command of battalion	A.a.B.
"	"	10 a.m. – 3.30 pm	Lively activity of enemy artillery on our front and support lines; no damage.	A.a.B
"	"	8.30 pm – 12.30 am	Working parties as on previous evening	A.a.B
"	"	9 pm	Draft of 63 Other Ranks joined Battalion in trenches.	A.a.B.

INTELLIGENCE SUMMARY

(Erase heading not required.)

Instructions regarding Summaries are contained in F. S. Regs., Part II. and the Staff Manual respectively. Title Pages will be prepared in manuscript.

Place	Date	Hour	Summary of Events and Information	Remarks and references to Appendices
WULVERGHEM	27th		Very quiet day	a.a.3.
"	"	8.30pm–11.30pm	Relief of companies in front line turned by companies in support. Work carried on afr relief on DIAGONAL and MOB LANE. Enemy machine gun and snipers active during the night.	a.a.3.
"	28		Enemy quiet during the day.	a.a.3
"	"	10.0am	G.O.C. 104th Division visited our trenches	a.a.3
"	"	9.30pm–11.30pm	Working parties on MOB LANE and DIAGONAL	a.a.3
"	29	10.0am	Gas alarms heard some distance to our right. Enemy attacked our division on our right. Precautionary measures taken but no gas reached our front. Enemy on our front quiet.	a.a.3.
"	"	—	Quiet day	a.a.3
"	"	8.30pm–12.30am	Working parties on DRAGON ALLEY, BOWLES LANE and SURREY LANE	a.a.3

INTELLIGENCE SUMMARY

(Erase heading not required.)

Instructions regarding War Diaries and Intelligence Summaries are contained in F.S. Regs., Part II. and the Staff Manual respectively. Title Pages will be prepared in manuscript.

Place	Date	Hour	Summary of Events and Information	Remarks and references to Appendices
WULVERGHEM	30th	3.15 am	Enemy released gas on our front. The first warning was heard from Bn on our right and a few minutes later the Brigade on our left. This was followed immediately by a report of gas from our left Company in C.O. Bde. H.Q. was at once informed. The gas cloud lasted from 15 to 20 minutes in various places. This was followed by a heavy barrage of shells of all calibre (and including gas-shells) on all routes of communication to the front-line. Places particularly noted were the MIDLAND DEFENCES, BOYLES FARM and the MESSINES — WULVERGHEM road. Bn HQ and support companies went to their battle position as laid down in defence scheme. Communication was maintained with Fwd Coys by telephone throughout the battle with exception of short period when Fwd Coy to Bn battle line. Enemy shelled front-line trench particularly left Coy but majority of shells dropped behind the trench causing little damage. No enemy infantry attack was made beyond the attempt to reach our right listening post. In this the enemy was effectively held up by our wire and in their attempt to cut it one German Officer and two men were thrown off by our men with bombs and rifle fire. The remainder of the party were eventually driven off.	OAB

INTELLIGENCE SUMMARY

(Erase heading not required.)

Instructions regarding War Diaries and Intelligence Summaries are contained in F.S. Regs., Part II and the Staff Manual respectively. Title Pages will be prepared in manuscript.

Place	Date	Hour	Summary of Events and Information	Remarks and references to Appendices
WULVERGHEM	30th	Dusk to daylight	As dawn broke the whole situation gradually died down and the possibility of a deliberate enemy attack being impossible the support coys and Bn H.Q. returned to their normal positions.	A.a.B
"	"	3 am	Both aircraft extremely active preventing enemy aeroplanes from reconnoitring. Action of gas effect, bombardment and evacuation of wounded and general chaos.	A.a.B
"	"	8am –1pm	Extremely quiet day on both sides. Enemy apparently in need of respiration and rest as ourselves.	A.a.B
"	"	2.30pm	Working parties to repair damage by shell fire & Royal Engineers to renew parapets and parapets 142 trench previous to relief.	A.a.B
"	"	9.45pm	Relief commenced by 1/4 R. Northampton Regt.	A.a.B
"	"	"	Enemy alarm signal on our left again witnessed as before & left Brigade accompanied by heavy shelling by ??? gas shells and S.O.S. trailings	A.a.B

1875. Wt. W593/826 1,000,000 4/15 J.B.C. & A. A.D.S.S./Forms/C. 2118.

INTELLIGENCE SUMMARY

(Erase heading not required.)

Instructions regarding War Diaries and Intelligence Summaries are contained in F.S. Regs, Part II. and the Staff Manual respectively. Title Pages will be prepared in manuscript.

Place	Date	Hour	Summary of Events and Information	Remarks and references to Appendices
WULVERGHEM	3rd	9.40 pm	Relief position for that Wk. D.C.L.I. by Bedf Regt taking over and Wiltshires officers & Coys and patrols which had been relieved were enquiring as to events at WULVERGHEM.	OaB
"	"	10 pm	Returned Wiltshire patrol (Lt Biffey) sent out to investigate the matter reported by Wiltshires. Gained no casualties or previous night and if possible to recover bodies or identification. It reported that our wire was still intact but large slabs of blood could be seen outside our wire and close to it besides the hedge. They also showed a German patrol leaving their trench and watching them under cover returned and directed Lewis gun fire on the spot enquired at.	OaB
"	"	11.45 pm	Relief of Bn Completed and proceeded to Camp at KORTE. PYP	to OaB

INTELLIGENCE SUMMARY

(Erase heading not required.)

Place	Date	Hour	Summary of Events and Information	Remarks and references to Appendices
WULVERGHEM			The casualties of the Bn during the tour 24th – 30th April were Officers, wounded 4; Ranks 1: Other ranks killed 6, wounded 44; gassed 19. Total Officers 5 Other ranks 42.	aa/3

J.H. Wilkinson Lt.M.
Comdg Leinster Regt.

73rd Brigade.
24th Division.

2nd BATTALION

LEINSTER REGIMENT.

May 1916.

D.H.Q.
  3rd Echelon

        Herewith Original War
Diary May 1916.
      It is regretted the
forwarding of this was overlooked owing
to move of Battalion in June.

                              A.A.Burns Lt
                                for Capt
13/7/16.   Comdg Leinster Regt

Divisional Routine Order
of 9th May 1916.

"SPECIAL ORDER"

The Commander of the 2nd Army has expressed a wish to convey to the Units engaged during the recent gas attack on this front his appreciation of the steadiness and courage displayed by all ranks, whereby the enemy failed to obtain any advantage from Gas Emission.

In communicating the above, the Corps Commander would like to express his appreciation of the high soldierly qualities shown by all ranks under the very trying circumstances.

Army Form C. 2118

2 Leinster Regt

Vol 77

WAR DIARY or INTELLIGENCE SUMMARY
(Erase heading not required.)

Place	Date 1916 May	Hour	Summary of Events and Information	Remarks and references to Appendices
KORTEPYP	1-6	—	In Bn. reserve at KORTEPYP Camp. Training carried out daily, and some working parties on cable burying by day.	
"	2	—	Leave to Ireland suspended on account of rebellion there.	A.9 hr
"	—	4 pm	Major R. ORPEN-PALMER rejoined Bn and took over command.	A.9 hr
"	4	4 pm	Lieut E.J. MAGNER, 3rd Bn., joined & posted to A Coy.	A.9 hr
"	5	10 pm	Lieut-Colonel G. BULLEN-SMITH rejoined Bn. and took over command	A.9 hr
"	6	9 pm	Bn. left camp by coys and relieved 4/NORTHANTS in trenches. Relief complete by 10.15 pm.	A.9 hr
WULVERGHEM	6-12	—	A quiet tour. Hostile artillery far greater than usual. Enemy's machine guns were always extra at nights from direction of ONTARIO and BIRTHDAY FARMS. Our artillery fired on several occasions and were effective in temporarily putting down the enemy guns. Considerable work was done by us on the DIAGONAL, on Cmn. trenches and on a new support trench near DRAGOON ALLEY in rear of the salient at 140 and 141.	
"	9	—	Following other at ordinary was received. A special congratulatory order passing the regt. on the Success in the recent gas attack was sent by the G.O.C. and Corps and published in Bde. orders.	Copy attached A.9 hr

WAR DIARY
or
INTELLIGENCE SUMMARY

(Erase heading not required.)

Army Form C. 2118

Place	Date	Hour	Summary of Events and Information	Remarks and references to Appendices
WULVERGHEM	12	12.10 a.m.	Lieut. L.D. BAILEY severely wounded.	A.9h.
"	"	11.30 p.m.	Relieved by 4/NORTHANTS and returned to RED LODGE. Casualties during tour 6-12-14 killed, 11 wounded.	A.9h.
RED LODGE	12-18	—	Bn. in Bde. reserve. Furnished working parties of about 420 men nightly.	
"	15	10 a.m.	Lieut-Col. G.M. BULLEN-SMITH, D.S.O left Bn. to take over command of the 5th Inf. Bde. Major R.A.H. ORPEN-PALMER assumed command of Bn.	A.9h.
"	17	3 p.m.	Captain R.C. METGE and K.B. O'MORCHOE and 2 Lieuts R. O'CONNOR and MORAN joined Bn.	A.9h.
"	"	8.30 p.m.	"Gas Alert" received.	A.9h.
"	18	12.15 a.m.	Gas alarms heard on or near front of division on our right but no signs of gas observed or reported.	A.9h.
WULVERGHEM	"	11.30 p.m.	Relieved 4/NORTHANTS in trenches.	A.9h.
"	20	—	Received notification that in future tours in trenches would be for eight days instead of six.	A.9h.
"	21	11.45 a.m.	"Gas Alert" cancelled.	A.9h.
"	23	1.10 p.m.	Gas Alert received.	A.9.B

Army Form C. 2118

WAR DIARY
or
INTELLIGENCE SUMMARY
(Erase heading not required.)

Place	Date May	Hour	Summary of Events and Information	Remarks and references to Appendices
NULVERGHEM	24th	6.30pm	Gas Alert - cancelled	aa/3
"	"	9.0pm	2/Lt H.H. THORNLEY joined the Battn	aa/3
"	"	6.30pm	Gas Alert - received	aa/3
"	25	12.45pm	Gas Alert - cancelled	aa/3
"	26	9.30pm	Battn relieved by 7th Northamptonshire Regt and proceeded to Camp at KORTEPYP. (Found working party of 150 men)	aa/3
KORTEPYP	27th	—	Inspections of arms & equipment & bathing of men	aa/3
"	"	8.30am	Working party of 150 men required for work behind Right sectn.	aa/3
"	28-31st		Training programme carried on - 5 hours daily under various subjects.	aa/3
"	"	6.30pm	Working parties nightly of 150 men required for work behind front line	aa/3
"	31st	3 am	Capt. S.E.B. Laville rejoined from sick leave	aa/3

WAR DIARY
or
INTELLIGENCE SUMMARY

Army Form C. 2118

Place	Date	Hour	Summary of Events and Information	Remarks and references to Appendices
KEMMEL	29th May	10.30am	The G.O.C. 2nd Army Sir H. Plumer presented medal ribbons to the undermentioned ranks:-	AAB
			LIEUT. A.A. BURNS := Distinguished Conduct Medal	
			7644 RSM SMITH := " " "	
			9894 Cpl CONNOLLY := " " "	AAB
			9291 L/Cpl REGAN := " " "	
			4215 " MORRISEY Military Medal	
			8030 Pte READ " "	
			9954 " SMITH " "	
			The last tour in the trenches was fairly quiet. Enemys artillery moderately active and did a small amount of damage to our trenches but few casualties were due to his artillery. Machine guns were active after dusk but our artillery checked this on any occasion when called upon, especially when work was hindered by this annoyance. Considerable amount of work was done by the Batt during this eight days in every portion allotted to Coys. Our casualties during the tour were killed other ranks 4. Wounded other ranks 20.	AAB
			R. Upher Palmer Major	
			Cmdg 2nd Lincoln Regt	

73rd Brigade.
24th Division.

2nd BATTALION

LEINSTER REGIMENT.

June 1916.

Army Form C. 2118

2 Leinster Regt

Vol 23

WAR DIARY
or
INTELLIGENCE SUMMARY
(Erase heading not required.)

Place	Date June	Hour	Summary of Events and Information	Remarks and references to Appendices
KORTEPYP	1		One Company and specialists at training. Working party 240 men by night on support lines and assembly trenches.	AA8 AA13
"	2		Reinforcement of 12 other ranks arrived.	AA8
"	"		Lt. W. H. Lorrie joined Battn. from the Base. Working party as on previous night	AA8
"	3	11.40 am	The Battn. had a test "Stand To." Battn. and 1st line Transport ready 15 men in 25 minutes.	AA8
"	"	9.30 pm	Battn. relieved 4th Rutland Regt. in left sector of trenches: A & C Coys in front-line B & D Coys in support.	AA8 AA13
KULVERGHEM	"		In the King's Birthday Honours the following were awarded to Battn: Major R. Q. Bryan Palmer (Comdg Battn.): Distinguished Service Order. A/RSM W. Kerrigan A Coy: Distinguished Conduct Medal. 9842 Cpl. P. Mahon HQ Signals: Military Medal	AA8 AA8 AA8
"	4	3 am	Capt. G. Murray "A" Coy killed by machine-gun fire. Capt. O'Keeffe took command of "A" Coy.	AA8 AA8
"	5		Reinforcement of 8 other ranks joined Battn.	AA8

Army Form C. 2118

WAR DIARY
or
INTELLIGENCE SUMMARY
(Erase heading not required.)

Instructions regarding War Diaries and Intelligence Summaries are contained in F.S. Regs., Part II. and the Staff Manual respectively. Title Pages will be prepared in manuscript.

Place	Date June	Hour	Summary of Events and Information	Remarks and references to Appendices
WULVERGHEM	7	6 pm	Reinforcement of 12 other ranks joined Batt. 2/Lieut R.H. SANDERS joined Batt.	AA3
"	"	9.30 pm / 12 m.n.	A & C Coys relieved in front line trenches by B & D Coys.	AA3
"	9		Lieut M.P. McNAMARA joined Batt.	AA3
"	10		2/Lt R.E. WARNER & 2/Lt H. POOLE joined Batt.	AA3
"	11	11.30 pm	Batt. relieved in the trenches by 7/Northants Regt & proceeded to RED LODGE (Brigade reserve). During the tour B & D Batt. had the enemy artillery were fairly active causing a moderate amount of damage to our trenches but not inflicting many casualties. The first 3 days were noted by an absence of artillery activity. On the fourth day it shelled heavily GRATON FARM and HIGGINSON AVENUE destroying the cover on the latter for some distance. Following day C2 was shelled with whizz-bangs & shrapnel causing a few casualties from the number. It shelled C2 & D 1 H 1 & 1 H 2 at intervals daily. On the 10th inst our 9.2 in guns mainly shelled ONTARIO FARM with great effect. The enemy retaliated with shell rifle Grenades & Trench Mortars. Their aerial Torpedo damage except in one place (DIAGONAL) where the Trench	AA3

1875. Wt. W593/826 1,000,000 4/16 J.W.C. & A. A.D.S.S./Forms/C. 2118.

WAR DIARY

or

INTELLIGENCE SUMMARY

(Erase heading not required.)

Army Form C. 2118

Place	Date	Hour	Summary of Events and Information	Remarks and references to Appendices
WULVERGHEM	3rd/11th		Bombing patrol requisited a scout hut destroying the trench for some distance. Machine Gun fire was as usual active at night. The casualties during this period were 6 Other Ranks killed 6 Wounded & 9. Officers killed 1 wounded k.d.	A.a.B
RED LODGE	12	8.0 p.m.	Batt. in Brigade reserve	a.a.B
"	"		Working party curtailed owing to heavy rain 15 180 men	a.a.B
"	"		3 Other ranks joined Batt.	a.a.B
"	14	11 am	Daylight saving scheme Time advanced one hour. 2/Lt W.M. Powell joined Batt.	a.a.B
"	15		Received Operation Orders entering the move of Batt. from this section	a.a.B
"	16	12.45 pm	Relieved in RED LODGE by the 26th Bn Australian Infantry whose Batt is taking over this section and marched to billets in LOCRE (BADAJOS HUTS).	pencil note below, Satt relieved
LOCRE	19	1 am	Batt got order to "STAND TO". Heavy shelling heard on 42nd Bde front	a.a.B
"	"	2.30 am	And released again	a.a.B
"	"	9 am	Order received to "stand down". Recce on "Gas alert" Officers & N.C.O's reconnoitred KEMMEL DEFENCES.	a.a.B a.a.B

WAR DIARY
or
INTELLIGENCE SUMMARY

(Erase heading not required.)

Army Form C. 2118

Place	Date June	Hour	Summary of Events and Information	Remarks and references to Appendices
LOCRE	14th	6 p.m.	2/Lt AM JAMIESON and 23 other ranks joined Battn.	aa13
"	16	8. a.m.	The Battn relieved 1st/6th Bn of 2nd Cavalry Division occupying KEMMEL defences and the Curtsy Officer (Lt-Col R.A.O.PALMER) took temporary command of whole defence.	aa13
"	"	"	The following dispositions were made: "B", "C" & "D" Coys moved to VANCOUVER Camp & "A" Coy remained in LOCRE providing guards control and frontier posts.	aa13
"	"	"	Battn. H.Q. remained in LOCRE	aa13
"	"	"	2 Lts E.P. HALL and H.V.T. FRENCH joined Battn.	aa13
"	19	3.0 p.m.	Battn moved to KEMMEL Shelters in relief of 5th YORKS and became BRIGADE reserve Battn.	aa13
KEMMEL SHELTERS	20		Reinforcement of 28 other ranks joined Battn.	aa13
KEMMELSHELTERS	20	12 M.N	Battn relieved 4th YORKS in front line left sector opposite WYSCHAETE	aa13
WYSCHAETE	"		The line taken over by the Battn stretches northward from the KEMMEL-WYSCHAETE road the right flank of Battn resting on N side of road. The trenches till are on the forward portion of a ridge which could be approached fairly well under cover. Enemy trenches are at sniping distance from within 60 yards to over 200 yards on the left. Two Companies occupy the front line garrison with one company in support at	aa13

1875 Wt. W593/826 1,000,000 4/17 v.B. & A. A.D.S.S./Forms/C. 2118.

WAR DIARY or INTELLIGENCE SUMMARY

Army Form C. 2118

Place	Date	Hour	Summary of Events and Information	Remarks and references to Appendices
WSCHAETE	June 20		S.P. 10 and S.P. 11 and no Company in reserve in KEMMEL CHATEAU. Behind the front line is constructed a system of strong Points further in rear in line of disconnected posts and so reserve line. The whole line is covered by one main communication trench with offshoots running up from it.	A.&B
"	21	9 am	Capt/Lt S.L.L. JOHNSTON severely wounded in head	A.&B
"	21	3.5pm	Capt/Lt S.L.L. JOHNSTON died of wounds in 2nd F.C. clearing station BAILLEUL	A.&B
"	"	1pm	LIEUT. H.T. POOLE took command of "C" Company	S.&B
"	"		Capt/Lt FREND joined the Battn from the Base	A.&B
"	22	9.15pm	"S.O.S." Alert received	A.&B
"	23	7.30pm	S.O.S. Alert cancelled	A.&B
"	24/25	10pm/4am	Relief of Companies in front line by support and reserve Company	A.&B
"	"	5 am	S.O.S. Alert	A.&B
"	"	7.30pm	S.O.S Alert cancelled	A.&B
"	"	10.30pm	LIEUT G.A. TODD joined from Hospital	A.&B

Army Form C. 21

WAR DIARY
or
INTELLIGENCE SUMMARY

(Erase heading not required.)

Instructions regarding War Diaries and Intelligence Summaries are contained in F.S. Regs., Part II. and the Staff Manual respectively. Title Pages will be prepared in manuscript.

Place	Date	Hour	Summary of Events and Information	Remarks and references to Appendices
WYSCHAETE	25	10.45pm	Our right company relieved in front line trenches by a company of 4th YORKS to facilitate their arrangement for a minor enterprise.	AA3
"	26	4pm	2/Lieut. A.J. DOBBIE joined the Battn.	AA3
"	27	1am	Raid on enemy trenches by detachment of 4th Yorks after artillery preparation.	AA3
"	29		16 other ranks joined Battn.	
"	28	12.40am	Battn. relieved in trenches by 7th Northumb'ld Regt. on relief Bn. proceeded to camp at WAKEFIELD HUTS near LOCRE. Battn. was in Divisional Reserve.	AA3
"			During the last time in trenches the enemy shelled our front trenches at intervals with Whizzbangs. He also used Trench Mortar bombs and Rifle Grenades frequently. Our Artillery were very active during the whole time and used also many effective in their retaliation. Sniping was quite normal and machine gun fire active at certain points. Our casualties during the period 20th-24th were, Officers killed nil; Wounded (since died one) Other ranks killed 4; Wounded 42; Wounded (at duty) 1 accidentally wounded 2. Total killed 4, died of wounds 1, Wounded 45.	AA3

WAR DIARY
or
INTELLIGENCE SUMMARY
(Erase heading not required.)

Army Form C. 2118

Place	Date	Hour	Summary of Events and Information	Remarks and references to Appendices
MAKEFIELD HO	28	2-2.30pm	Provided working party of 300 men for Divisional dispatch Corps	aa/3
"	"	9.30pm	4 other ranks joined Batt.	aa/3
"	29	2.0pm	Working party of 350 men for signal corps	aa/3
"	"	10.20pm	Batt. received orders to "STAND TO" ready to move in twenty-five minutes	aa/3
"	"	11.15	Batt. ordered to STAND DOWN	aa/3
"	30	"	Capt. R.G. METGE to Hospital	aa/3
"	"	4pm	2/Lt H.T.P. SIDDONS and 19 other ranks joined the Batt.	aa/3

R. Alpher Colvin
Lieut Colonel
Cmdg 2/ Lincoln Regt.

S E C R E T.

HEADQUARTERS 73rd BDE.
No. B.M. 194.
Date 15. 6. 16.

Officer Commanding

      2nd. Leinster Regiment.
      9th. Royal Sussex Regiment.
      7th. Northamptonshire Regiment.
      13th. Middlesex Regiment.

The 73rd. Infantry Brigade will relieve the 150th Infantry Brigade in the line nights 19/20 and 20/21st June, and the following will be the moves:-

19th. June.
7th. Northamptonshire Regt. from HAEGEDOORNE to LOCRE
                                                   (WAKEFIELD HUTS)

Night 19/20th June.
13th. Middlesex Regt. from WAKEFIELD HUTS to Right
                                          Section Trenches.
2nd. Leinster Regt. from BADAJOZ HUTS to KEMMEL Shelters.

20th. June.
9th. Royal Sussex Regt. from ST. JANS CAPPEL to
                                         WAKEFIELD HUTS.

Night 20/21 June.
2nd. Leinster Regt. from KEMMEL Shelters to Left Section
                                                       Trenches.
7th. Northamptonshire Regt from WAKEFIELD HUTS to
                                              KEMMEL Shelters.

Operation orders will be issued in due course.

R. Hoswell.

H.Q. 73rd. I.B.   Major,
15. 6. 16.   Brigade Major, 73rd. Infantry Brigade.

SECRET.   COPY No:- 9

73rd. INFANTRY BRIGADE.

OPERATION ORDER NO. 45.

H.Q. 73 I.B. June 15th. 1916.

1.   The 73rd. Infantry Brigade will be relieved in the Centre Sector by the 7th. Australian Brigade as per attached tables.

2.   One Officer per company and 1 N.C.O. per platoon of the 25th. and 26th. battalions of the 7th. Australian Brigade will go into the trenches tomorrow and stay there till the arrival of their battalion.
        Details of other advanced parties have already been notified.

3.   The reliefs of the trench wardens of Forts BRANDON and EBERLE will be found by the 28th. battalion and will arrive with the 26th. Battalion tomorrow.

4.   Units will hand over to corresponding units of the 7th. Australian Brigade:-
        All Trench Stores.
        Trench Maps (including Sheet 28 S.W.4 (1/10,000).
        Defence Schemes.
        Log Books.
        Intelligence Reports.
        Tables of work in hand and proposed.
        All documents and information which may be of
                                                    value.

        Lists of Trench Stores and documents handed over will be forwarded to Brigade Headquarters within 48 hours of relief being completed.

5.   Arrangements for Transport of surplus stores and the position of refilling points will be notified later.

6.   The command of the Centre Sector will pass to B.G.C., 7th. Australian Brigade on completion of Infantry Reliefs night 17th./18th. June.

7.   Please acknowledge.

ISSUED AT 12 noon.   R Hewlett
                                                    Major,
                        Brigade Major, 73rd. Infantry Brigade.

        Copy No. 1. File.
                 2. War Diary.
                 3. "G" 24th. Div.
                 4. "Q" 24th. Div.
                 5. 17 I.B.
                 6. 72 I.B.
                 7. 7th. Australian Brigade.
                 8. 150th. I.B.
                 9. 2nd. Leinster Regt.
                10. 9th. Royal Sussex Regt.
                11. 7th. Northamptons.
                12. 13th. Middlesex Regt.
                13. 73rd. Coy. Machine Gun Corps.
                14. 73rd. Trench Mortar Battery.
                15. A.P.M. 24 Div.

RELIEF OF THE 73rd. INFANTRY BRIGADE BY THE 7th. AUSTRALIAN BRIGADE.

7th. AUSTRALIAN BRIGADE.

DATE.	UNIT.	FROM.	TO.	ROUTE.	REMARKS.
16th. June.(1).	26th. Bn.	2nd. ANZAC Div. Area.	RED LODGE.	LE ROMARIN T.27.b. 8.0 - T.28.b.5.9 - T.22.d.2.5 - RED LODGE.	Guides from H.Q. 73 I.B meet coys. at LE ROMARIN at 11.30 a.m.
	7th.Aus.M.G. Coy.	"	T.22.b.1.1.	LE ROMARIN.	Guides from 73rd. Coy. M.G.Corps meet coy. at LE ROMARIN at 12.noon.
	7th. Aus. T.M.Batt.	"	T.21.b.2.5.	"	Guides from 73 T.M.Battery meet battery at LE ROMARIN at 12.15 p.m.
	25th. Batt.	"	KORTEPYP.	B.1. central - T.20.c.3.0 - KORTEPYP.	Guides from 13th. Middlesex meet coys. at B.1. central 11.30 a.m.
Night 16th/17th. June. (2).	7th. Aus.M.G. Coy.(12 guns)	T.22.b.1.1. Trench area.			All arrangements for relief to be made between O.'s.C. M.G.Coys. direct.
17th. June. (3).	28th. Bn.	2nd. ANZAC Div. Area.	RED LODGE.	As in (1).	Guides from 73rd. Bde. H.Q. meet coys. at LE ROMARIN at 9.30 p.m.
	27th.Bn.	"	KORTEPYP.	As in (1).	Guides from 73rd. Bde. H.Q. will meet coys at B.1. central at 5 p.m.
Night 17/18th. June. (4).	26th. Bn.	RED LODGE.	RIGHT SECTION TRENCHES(136 - 140).	Via T.18.a.4.7.	First coy. to pass T.18.a.4.7. at 10 p.m. O.C. 9th. Royal Sussex to arrange direct with O.C. 26th. Bn. re guides.
	25th. Bn.	KORTEPYP.	Left Section Trenches (141 C.2.)	Via NEUVE EGLISE - WULVERGHEM.	To be clear of KORTEPYP by 6 p.m. but not to pass NEUVE EGLISE till 9.45 p.m. Guides for coys. from KORTEPYP to WULVERGHEM will be provided by 73rd. Bde. H.Q. O.C. 7th. Northamptons will arrange for guides from that point to trenches.

NOTE. UNITS OF THE 7th. AUSTRALIAN BRIGADE WILL MOVE WHEN IN THE 24th. DIV AREA WITH AN INTERVAL OF 5 MINS. BETWEEN COYS.

RELIEF OF THE 73rd. INFANTRY BRIGADE BY 7th. AUSTRALIAN BRIGADE.

73rd. INFANTRY BRIGADE.

DATE.	UNIT.	FROM.	TO.	ROUTE.	REMARKS.
16th. June.	2nd. Leinsters.	RED LODGE.	LOCRE (BADAJOZ HUTS.)	To B.1. central thence via S.27.a.6.7 - S.15.d.3.7½ - S.15.c.10.8 - S.9.b.3.0 - S.9.a.6.5 - LOCRE.	Not to leave until after arrival of corresponding battalions of 7th. Australian Brigade. These 2 battalions on arrival at LOCRE will come under tactical orders of G.O.C. KEMMEL DEFENCES (H.Q. at LOCRE) Advanced parties of 1 Officer & 4 N.C.O's per battalion will report at 159th. I.B. H.Q. at LOCRE by 12 noon 16th. Inst.
	13th. Middlesex	KORTE PYP.	LOCRE (WAKEFIELD HUTS)	DO.	
17th. June.	73rd. M.G.Coy.	T.22.b.1.1.	Will be notified.		
	73rd. T.M.Batt'y.	T.21.b.2.5.	do.		
Night 17/18th. June.	9th. R. Sussex. Right Section	ST.JANS CAPPEL. Trenches.		B.1. central - BAILEUL- ST.JANS CAPPEL.	Billetting parties will meet Staff Captain tomorrow morning at a place and time to be notified.
	7th. Northamptons. Left Section	HAEGDOORNE. Trenches.		B.1. central - S.27.a.6.7 - S.15.d.3.7½ - S.15.c.10. 8 - HAEGDOORNE.	do.

15. 6. 16.

73rd Inf.Bde.
24th Div.

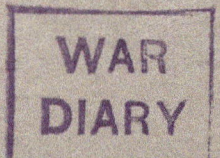

2nd BATTN. THE PRINCE OF WALES'S' LEINSTER REGIMENT
(ROYAL CANADIANS).

J U L Y

1 9 1 6

WAR DIARY or INTELLIGENCE SUMMARY

(Erase heading not required.)

Place	Date JULY	Hour	Summary of Events and Information	Remarks and references to Appendices
LOCRE	1	9 am	Bn provided working party of 150 men for Divisional Signal Corps	AA/3
"	"	10 "	Sunday Parade service at LOCRE Chapel	AA/3
"	2	10 am	Working party of 150 men for Signal Corps. Capt. R.G. METGE invalided to United Kingdom	AA/3
"	3	9 am	Working party of 150 men for Signal Corps	AA/3
"	"	11 pm	Relieved 4th Northampton Regt in trenches. Line held now slightly modified, length of front being smaller. Recon Company & outflies are now located at Curral in KEMMEL Shelters. "C" Company went into front line trench with one platoon of A Company on their left. "D" Company and two platoons of "B" Coy at KEMMEL Shelters. A Company 3 platoons SP III (Support Coy).	AA/3
WYSCHAETE Trenches	6	4.30 pm	Draft of 40 other ranks joined Batt.	AA/3
"	7	11.30 pm	B Company relieved A Coy in front line & support line trenches	AA/3
"	8	11.30 pm	Owing to removal of 42nd Bde from this sector the Batt. was relieved by the	AA/3

INTELLIGENCE SUMMARY

(Erase heading not required.)

Instructions regarding War Diaries and Intelligence Summaries are contained in F.S. Regs., Part II. and the Staff Manual respectively. Title Pages will be prepared in manuscript.

Place	Date July	Hour	Summary of Events and Information	Remarks and references to Appendices
WYSCHAETE	8	4.15pm	4th YORKS Regt 150th Bde 50th Division, one Generals to Camp in DONCASTER Hub LOCRE (Operation order attached) Our Casualties during the period 3rd – 9th inst. were – Other Ranks killed 2; Wounded 23; Total 25	aa 8 aa 8
LOCRE	9		2/Lt M.E. SHARPE joined Bn on transfer from 5th R.I. Lancers	aa 8
"	"		2/Lt H.M. CLANCY joined Bn from 3rd Batn.	aa 8
"	10	9 am	Working Party of 305 men under R.E. in KEMMEL hill.	aa 8
"	"	9 pm	Working Party of 350 men under R.E.	aa 8
"	11	5.30 am	Batln. marched to BULFORD Camp + became Brigade Reserve Regt. (See operation orders attached)	aa 8
BULFORD CP	12	9.30 am	Two Companies B & D marched to RIDGE Wood aux. FARM T3 c J 9½ and they were detailed	aa 6
"	"		for work daily under C.R.A	
"	13	10	Specialist training.	aa 8
"	"	9 pm	150 men provided by Bn to work under R.E	aa 8
"	14	9am-5pm	Training of Specialists – under R.E. Platoon drill	aa 8
"	"	9 pm	150 men working under R.E. arrangements.	aa 13

INTELLIGENCE SUMMARY

(Erase heading not required.)

Instructions regarding War Diaries and Intelligence Summaries are contained in F.S. Regs., Part II. and the Staff Manual respectively. Title Pages will be prepared in manuscript.

Place	Date July	Hour	Summary of Events and Information	Remarks and references to Appendices
BULFORD CP.	15	9 am	Training	AA13
"	"	9 pm – 2 am	245 NCOs & S. Officers employed carrying gas cylinders to various hiveh. allotted on MESSINES — WYSCHAETE front.	AA13
"	16	9 am	Training of specialists	AA13
"	"	9 pm – 2 am	300 NCOs & S. Officers carrying gas cylinders to same system of hiveh as previous night	AA13
"	17	2.30 pm	GAS ALERT	AA13
"	"	3.22 "	Gas alert cancelled	AA13
"	"	9 pm	All working parties cancelled in view of minor enterprise to be carried out on our front. Heavy bombardment of enemy line on our front.	AA13
"	18	11 am		
"	18	12.40 pm	GAS ALERT	AA13
"	19	8.30	Orders received by Bn to be in readiness to move by 2 pm	AA13

INTELLIGENCE SUMMARY

(Erase heading not required.)

Instructions regarding War Diaries and Intelligence Summaries are contained in F.S. Regs., Part II. and the Staff Manual respectively. Title Pages will be prepared in manuscript.

Place	Date	Hour	Summary of Events and Information	Remarks and references to Appendices
BULFORD CP	19	11 am	Order confirmed and the Batt. detailed to move by Buses at 10 pm to billets in METEREN area. Division being relieved by 20 7th Division	aa/3.
"	"	10 pm	Bn. moved by Bus after being relieved by 10th KINGS Regt. 61st Bde. Batt. got off buses in FLETRE and marched about 2 miles to billets in farms. Bn. H.Q. at HOGEDORNfarm Q 23.a.3.5 (sheet 24)	aa/3.
HOGEDORN	20		Inspection & Training during afternoon	aa.3
"	21	4 am	Bn. received instruction to be ready to move at short notice & all surplus kits to be stored in BAILLEUL.	aa.3
"	"		2nd Lieut R.E. KARNER admitted to Hospital	aa.3
"	22		Training: Physical drill, bayonet fighting, bomb, & Lewis Gunnery	aa.3
"	23		Training: Lieut A.C.S. PALIN and 2/Lieut F.C. HITCHCOCK joined from base	aa.3

INTELLIGENCE SUMMARY

(Erase heading not required.)

Instructions regarding War Diaries and Intelligence Summaries are contained in F. S. Regs., Part II. and the Staff Manual respectively. Title Pages will be prepared in manuscript.

Place	Date July	Hour	Summary of Events and Information	Remarks and references to Appendices
HUGEDORM	24	2.4 pm	Batt. entrained and railed to SALEUX, S.W. of AMIENS arriving there 1 am	a.a./3
SALEUX	26	1.30 am	Bn marched to billets in village of MOLLIENS VIDAME about 11 miles west of detraining station.	a.a./3.
MOLLIENS– VIDAME	26		2nd Lieuts K.J. PORTER and M.F.Y. HAMILTON joined from Base.	a.a.8.
"	27	9.30 am 12.30 pm	Training of Coys in Running, Bayonet fighting etc. Inter section revolver & Lewis Gun.	a.a./3
"	28	4 am	Lt. A.P. FATELY joined Bn as a probation from A.S.C. 4 other ranks joined	a.a./3 a.a./3
"	29	9 – 1 pm	2nd Lt D.P.A. McCANN joined Bn from 4th Bn Leinster Regt. Training continued. Orders received to move. Operation orders attached	a.a.? a.a.?
"	30	1 pm	Bn paraded 5.30 am marched to HANGEST entrained and railed to VECQUEMONT arriving 3 pm. Marched to VAUX arriving 7.30 pm. Very hot day. Transport started 9.30 pm on night of 30/31st and marched by road	a.a.?
VAUX	31	9.30 pm		

R.P. [signature]
Lt. Colonel
Commanding 2nd Bn Leinster Regt

73rd Brigade.
24th Division

2nd BATTALION

LEINSTER REGIMENT.

September 1916.

Army Form C. 2118.

WAR DIARY
INTELLIGENCE SUMMARY.
(Erase heading not required.)

24

Vol 26

Place	Date	Hour	Summary of Events and Information	Remarks and references to Appendices
Independent Cavalry Brigade			As moved off September 1916 at Inversicorde Regiment	

INTELLIGENCE SUMMARY

(Erase heading not required.)

Place	Date	Hour	Summary of Events and Information	Remarks and references to Appendices
LONGUEVAL	Sept 1		Battalion now occupying left portion of our original front line. Endeavours to extend our position to the right by bombing were unsuccessful. Enemy in great strength about WOOD LANE and ORCHARD trench. At 9.50AM a new bombing attack made up PLUM STREET was unsuccessful. At 6.30pm an attack by 3rd R.B. recovered ORCHARD STREET. 2nd I/R A E O'CONNOR and 2nd Lt A M JAMESON killed and 2nd Lt W M POWELL and 2nd Lt A J DOBB 1st wounded	appx?
	2		Position as yesterday. Two companies now holding left of front line and support line. Two companies in support to right battalion. 2nd Lt D P McCANN wounded	
		10pm	Batt. then relieved by 2/BUFFS and 7/NORTHAMPTONS and returned to old trenches near MAMETZ	appx?

INTELLIGENCE SUMMARY

(Erase heading not required.)

Summaries are contained in F.S. Regs., Part II. and the Staff Manual respectively. Title Pages will be prepared in manuscript.

Place	Date Sept	Hour	Summary of Events and Information	Remarks and references to Appendices
MAMETZ	2		Total Casualties during period 31st to 2nd affair 2 killed 4 wounded. O. Ranks 30 killed 13 missing 114 wounded	accp
FRICOURT	4		Battalion marched from MAMETZ to camp near FRICOURT and	accp
DERNACOURT	5		Here we following afternoon to camp at DERNACOURT arriving there at 6 p.m. Inspection by G.O.C. 24th Division	accp
	6		Battalion entrained at 4 a.m at EDGE HILL Station DERNACOURT and detrained at — LONGPRÉ at 12 noon and marched to Billets at BRUCHAMPS	accp
BRUCHAMPS	7 8 9 10		Training in bomb throwing, bayonet fighting, coy in attack	accp
	11 12 13		Training	accp

INTELLIGENCE SUMMARY

(Erase heading not required.)

Place	Date	Hour	Summary of Events and Information	Remarks and references to Appendices
BRUCHAMPS	14		Battalion Sports	acap
	15 16 17 18		Training in Bombing, bayonet fighting, coy in attack, and night marching, route march.	acap
	19		Marched from BRUCHAMPS to LONGPRÉ. Entrained 9 p.m. and detraining at FOUQUERILLE and marched to billets in BRUAY	acap
BRUAY	20 21		In billets. parties of officers kept in buses to inspect front line near CLARENCY.	acap
	22		MARCHED to CAMBLAIN L'ABBÉ to relieve 7/SEAFORTHS. operation orders attached	acap
	23		Capt. E.C. BARRY received his MILITARY CROSS. N° 7218 L/Corp. J. MORRISEY and 8030 Pte P. REID received bars to their military medals N° 7974 Pte T. MERRIMAN received his Military medal	acap

INTELLIGENCE SUMMARY

(Erase heading not required.)

Place	Date	Hour	Summary of Events and Information	Remarks and references to Appendices
SOUCHEZ	Sept 23		Battalion relieved 4/S. AFRICAN SCOTTISH in front line trenches between VIMEY RIDGE and SOUCHEZ. Operation orders attached	app
	24 25 26		In trenches. Enemy's attitude of trench Quiet. 1st Proving through and communication trenches. Lieut H.C. BERNE to hospital sick	app
	27		Increased activity on the part of our Stokes mortars and trench mortars. Enemy's retaliation nil.	app
	28		More activity on our part. Two officers patrols during night. 2nd Lt C. SYKES found an Inspection short line indicated by G.O.C.	app
	29		A/7/NORTHAMPTONS Capt P.S. LYNCH found an outpost on Command of B. Coy. 2nd Lt T.E. HADDICK to hospital sick.	app
	30		One heavy gun ranged on Enemy trenches. Total casualties 23rd - 30th killed 3 wounded 8	app

A.J. Murphy, major
Commanding 3rd Leinster Regt

73rd Brigade.
24th Division

2nd BATTALION

LEINSTER REGIMENT.

October 1916.

INTELLIGENCE SUMMARY

(Erase heading not required.)

Army Form C.2118

October 1916

Place	Date October	Hour	Summary of Events and Information	Remarks and references to Appendices
DALY'S	1		Battalion relieved by 7th Bn Northamptn Regt and went back to Support Sector. Two Companies in the BAJOLLE Line and two Companies in CARENCY.	
	2,3,4,5,6		Working parties in front line and communication trenches, and carrying parties to Trench Mortar Batteries. I.O. and proposed marching Posts reconnoitred the area to be manned. 1 O.R. wounded	
	7		Lieut A.P. GATELY, 2nd Lieut D.H. McCANN and 29 men raided the German trenches. Known German Casualties 3 killed, 4 killed or wounded. 1 wounded prisoner of 101st R Saxon Regt. Own Casualties – Lieut A.P. GATELY wounded slightly, O.R. 1 died of wounds, 5 wounded. Detailed reports on raid attached in duplicate at copy. Lieut D.H. McCANN awarded the MILITARY CROSS	
	8		Working parties as usual.	
	9		Battalion ordered to move to Reserve Area. 1 O.R. wounded	
	10		Battalion relieved the 8th EAST Regiment WEST KENT Regt. 16 O.R. awarded the MILITARY MEDAL	
GOUY SERVINS	11		Training. Inspections, Rifle drill and Platoon drill. Lt A.P. GATELY to hospital. List attached	
	12		Training as above. 2nd Lt O.R. BRASSINGTON transferred to Royal Flying Corps.	
	13		Training as above. Major A.D. MURPHY on 10 days leave. Capt J. FREND assumed command of the Battalion	
	14,15		Training. Platoon drill, communication drill	

INTELLIGENCE SUMMARY

(Erase heading not required.)

Instructions regarding War Diaries and Intelligence Summaries are contained in F.S. Regs., Part II and the Staff Manual respectively. Title Pages will be prepared in manuscript.

Place	Date	Hour	Summary of Events and Information	Remarks and references to Appendices
GOUY SERVINS	15		Church Parade at 11 A.M.	acct?
	16		6. O.R. Joined. Training as usual	acct?
	17, 18		List 103 Major A.D MURPHY to be Temp. Lt. Colonel. 2nd Lieut F.C. HITCHCOCK to be Temp. Captain. Training.	acct?
BERTHONVAL	19		Battalion relieved the 1st Bn. NORTH STAFFORDSHIRE Regt in the right Sub-section of trenches. 3 O.R. awarded MILITARY MEDAL. 1 Lt. attached.	acct?
	20		Quiet day. Party of 9th R. SUSSEX Regt patrol in NO MAN'S LAND in front of our trenches. Unit & raid a raid.	
	21		50 O.R. joined Bn. No 3877 R.Q.M.S. VICKERY awarded MERITORIOUS MEDAL. Enemy's trench mortars active. Our artillery retaliated.	acct?
	22		22 O.R. joined Bn. - Trench Mortars again active - SUSSEX raid postponed. Colonel A.D MURPHY returned from leave and assumed Command. 4 O.R. joined Bn.	acct?
	23			
	24, 25, 26		Trench War activity. Our retaliation by our artillery. Gun machine gun's very active during the night. - 2nd Lt H.M. CLANCHY transferred to 73rd L.T.M. Battery.	acct?
CAMBLAIN L'ABBÉE	27		Battalion relieved by the 16th Bn. Canadian Scots and marched by platoons to hutments.	acct?
NOEUX-LES-MINES	28		Battalion relieved by the 5th Bn. Canadians and marched to billets in NOEUX-LES-MINES in the 40th Division area. 2nd Lieut H.W. NORMAN from the 7th Bn. and 2nd Lieut W.D. LAUDER from the 6th Bn. joined	acct?
	29		Battalion relieved M.A. FOLEY and 2nd Lieut W.D. LAUDER	acct?
MAROC	29		Battalion relieved the 19th Bn. R.W.F. in support in LOOS Sector.	acct?

INTELLIGENCE SUMMARY

(Erase heading not required.)

Instructions regarding War Diaries and Intelligence Summaries are contained in F.S. Regs., Part II. and the Staff Manual respectively. Title Pages will be prepared in manuscript.

Place	Date	Hour	Summary of Events and Information	Remarks and references to Appendices
MAROC	30		Quiet along the front; One Coy in DUKE STREET near LOOS and one Coy in SOUTH STREET. 1 Officer and 30 men in TRAVERS and St JAMES KEEPS remainder of Bn and H.Q. in MAROC. 21 O.R. sent to join 7th Bn. Bn mainly used for working parties	over
"	31		Bn mainly used for working parties	over

A J Murphy Lt Colonel
Commdg. 3rd Bn Tyneside Scottish Rgt

73rd Brigade.
24th Division.

2nd BATTALION

LEINSTER REGIMENT.

November 1916.

Army Form C. 2118.

WAR DIARY
or
INTELLIGENCE SUMMARY.
(Erase heading not required.)

Vol 28

War Diary

9th Leinster Regiment

For the month of

November 1916

Army Form C. 2118.

WAR DIARY
or
INTELLIGENCE SUMMARY.
(Erase heading not required.)

Instructions regarding War Diaries and Intelligence Summaries are contained in F. S. Regs., Part II. and the Staff Manual respectively. Title pages will be prepared in manuscript.

Place	Date	Hour	Summary of Events and Information	Remarks and references to Appendices
MAROC	November 3, 5, 6, 7		Battalion in support line, one coy in DUKE STREET near LOOS and one coy in O.G.1, one officer and 30 men in TRAVER'S and ST JAMES KEEPS. Remainder of battalion in MAROC. Battalion mainly used for working parties and carrying bombs for Trench Mortars. 1 O.R. wounded on 4th.	scaf?
"	8		Battalion relieved 7th Bn Northampton shire Regt. at 8 a.m. Two companies in front line, 1 officer and 36 men on the DOUBLE CRASSIER – One coy in left support and one coy less two platoons in right support. Two platoons in MAROC at the disposal of the Commanding Officer and used by front line coys for work at night.	aci?
	9		The attack on the Enemy was extremely quiet, no hostile shelling and very little rifle fire. Because of trench mortaring what was effectively shot out by our Stokes guns and artillery.	aci?
	10		At our request enemy's trenches near K.N. Craven were shelled during the afternoon. In the evening at 10 p.m. a large working party was dispersed by our guns. Reinforcements 26 O.R. joined.	aci?
	11		Reinforcements 26 O.R. joined. Enemy very quiet. Total casualties during tour 5 O.R.	

WAR DIARY or INTELLIGENCE SUMMARY

Army Form C. 2118.

Place	Date	Hour	Summary of Events and Information	Remarks and references to Appendices
MAROC	November 12		Battalion relieved by 7th Bn Northamptonshire Regt and became Battalion Reserve and went into billets in MAROC. Capt R.E.G. VAN CUTSEN joined Bn from 4th Bn and posted to D Coy.	
	13/14/15/16/17		Battalion rested by companies in the firing line and rest at the New Box Respirator. Battalion bathed in LES BREBIS booths - most of the work done during this period consisted of working and carrying parties for the front line Battalion, Tunnellers and R.E. Casualties 2 O.R. wounded. Reinforcements 6 O.R.	arr?
	18		Battalion relieved 1st Bn Northamptonshire Regt in the front line. Saint dispositions as previously. Reinforcements (vide War Diary October) drawn in with modest return	arr?
	19		By Corps Commander 2nd Lieut G. CAREY joined from 7th Battalion. Enemy more active. Trench mortars parked up. No damage done	arr?
	20/21/22		At 12:15 midnight Lieut PORTER and Bn Scouts carried out a Bangalore Torpedo, which was exploded on enemy's wire. This was followed by a general bombardment from our Trench mortars and artillery. Enemy reply was feeble. Casualties were found	
	23		19 — 23rd 2 O.R. killed. 6 O.R. wounded.	
	045		Battalion relieved by 7th Bn Northamptonshire Regt and became Reserve Support Battalion	arr?

Army Form C. 2118.

WAR DIARY
or
INTELLIGENCE SUMMARY.
(Erase heading not required.)

Instructions regarding War Diaries and Intelligence Summaries are contained in F. S. Regs., Part II. and the Staff Manual respectively. Title pages will be prepared in manuscript.

Place	Date	Hour	Summary of Events and Information	Remarks and references to Appendices
	November			
MAROC	24		One Coy in DUKE STREET and one Coy in DUGOUT ROW - This Coy also found garrison of two K2 pts. Two Coys in billets in MAROC. Battalion mainly employed in support duties and carrying. Reinforcements during this form 43 O.R. Casualties 3 O.R. wounded.	app 5
	25 26 27 28 29			
	30		Bn. relieved 15th Hampshire Regt and became in the front line. Dispositions as before.	app 3

A J Murphy, Lt Colonel
Commanding 2nd Bn. Leinster Regt.

73rd Brigade.
24th Division.

2nd BATTALION

LEINSTER REGIMENT

December 1916.

73rd Brigade.
24th Division.

Army Form C. 2118.

WAR DIARY
or
INTELLIGENCE SUMMARY.
(Erase heading not required.)

T332

Confidential

War Diary of
II Macedonian Regt
for
month of December
1916

Vol 29

WAR DIARY
or
INTELLIGENCE SUMMARY
(Erase heading not required.)

Army Form C. 2118.

Place	Date December	Hour	Summary of Events and Information	Remarks and references to Appendices
LOOS (front line)	1		Quiet day, two parties were out during the night reconnoitring a white flag hoisted out by the Enemy.	aaa?
	2		Officers patrol under Lieut. H.C. BERNE (M.C.) failure returned with but Lieut. BERNE who is missing.	aaa?
	3 & 4		Enemy artillery quiet, though their aerial observers were very active.	aaa?
	6		Enemy raided the left of our front line being easy in the morning, but were driven off with heavy loss. Our casualties were slight. 2/Lieut. C.J.H. MORITZ showing great gallantry to get with his servant Pte O'NEILL. He was killed and his servant wounded. One wounded German was captured. Total are casualties from the surprise: 1 Officer killed, 1 Officer wounded, 3 OR killed, 6 OR wounded. Details of attack attached.	

2449 Wt. W14957/M90 750,000 1/16 J.B.C. & A. Forms/C.2118/12.

WAR DIARY
or
INTELLIGENCE SUMMARY

Army Form C. 2118.

Place	Date	Hour	Summary of Events and Information	Remarks and references to Appendices
LOOS (Les Brebis)	6		Battalion relieved of the 7th Northampton Shire Regt. and gone to LES BREBIS as Divisional Support, leaving two platoons at MAROC. LIEUT N.P. LISTON returns to duty from leave.	aaop.
			The two Coys at MAROC employed at carrying to T.M. and wiring parties to R.E. T.M. and 7th Northants also employed upon building new Bn. H.Q. The Coys at LES BREBIS in training, route marches and platoon drills and wiring. Completing I.O.R. killed, 3 O.R. wounded. 5 O.R. joined Bn.	aaop.
	10	8pm	Bombardment 7.7mm Regt. North Hants along the frontline.	accoi.
(Mazingarbe)			Proceeding officers joined the Battalion on the 10th inst. 2nd Lieut A.E. AZIR.. A. NYE E.A. PRENDERGAST I.A. SMYTHEADY T.M. MACREADY THUNDER.	evens.

2449 Wt. W14957/M90 750,000 1/16 J.B.C. & A. Forms/C.2118/12.

WAR DIARY or INTELLIGENCE SUMMARY

Army Form C. 2118.

Place	Date	Hour	Summary of Events and Information	Remarks and references to Appendices
Loos (Front line)	December 12		The Bn relieved the 7th NORTHAMPTONSHIRE Regt in the frontline.	acs?
	13		Enemy's attitude fairly quiet, in exchange with bursts of aerial darts and enemy minenwerfers. 1 O.R. wounded on the 13th.	
	14			
	15		5 O.R. joined Bn on the 15th.	acs?
	16			
	17		The Bn relieved by the 7th NORTHAMPTONSHIRE Regt, Company HQ Bn in Bage Salford, 2nd Lieut C. SIKES wounded. 2 O.R. killed, and 1 O.R. wounded. Same day. 11 O.R. join the Bn.	
Bage, Salford	18		Enemy aeroplanes pried our camp but except our patrols & wiring hardly anything done. Weather fair.	acs?
	19			
	20			
	21		Enemy's Bn Enemy was quiet.	
	22		6 O.R. joined Bn.	
	23		Major J.J. FREEMAN joined Bn from the 3rd Bn.	acs?
	24		Bn Relieved 7th Northamptonshire Regt in front line.	

Army Form C. 2118.

WAR DIARY
or
INTELLIGENCE SUMMARY

(Erase heading not required.)

Place	Date	Hour	Summary of Events and Information	Remarks and references to Appendices
LOOS (trench line)	25		Enemy very quiet. Our artillery very active. 2 O.R. wounded.	Aag?
	26		Enemy still quiet. Our artillery bombarded hostile lines.	
	27		2 O.R. wounded. Capt P.S. LYNCH (M.E.) killed. Sgt. McCORMACK died of wounds & 2 O.R. wounded. All from the bursting of a Lewis Gun. about Otherwise enemy quiet.	Aa?
	28, 29		Weather very wet, enemy Enemy, our Stokes artillery active.	Aa?
LES BREBIS	30		Bn. relieved by the 1/7th. NORTHAMPTONSHIRE Bn. and went into Reserve. Weather very wet and ground very wet.	Aa?
	31		Pipe inspection.	

A.G Murphy. Lt Colonel
Commanding 1/5 Lincoln Regt.

Index..........................

SUBJECT.

No.	Contents.	Date.
	2nd. Bn: Leinster Regt Jany — Dec 1917.	

Army Form C. 2118.

WAR DIARY
or
INTELLIGENCE SUMMARY.

(Erase heading not required.)

73/674

Vol 30

Confidential

War Diary of
Leinster Regiment
for the month of
January 1917.

Place	Date	Hour	Summary of Events and Information	Remarks and references to Appendices

Instructions regarding War Diaries and Intelligence Summaries are contained in F. S. Regs., Part II. and the Staff Manual respectively. Title pages will be prepared in manuscript.

WAR DIARY or INTELLIGENCE SUMMARY

Army Form C. 2118.

Place	Date	Hour	Summary of Events and Information	Remarks and references to Appendices
LES BREBIS	Jan 1917 1/2/3		Inspections and Platoon Parades. 20 O.R. joined. On the night of the 3rd Sergt. W.O's and Sergeants had a dinner. The Commanding Officer spoke to them. Comp. Sergt. Major McNAMARA decorated with the D.C.M. by the B.G.C. No D. Coys Rect their dinner. 5 O.R. joined.	aca? aca?
	4		Bn. relieved the 7th Northamptonshire Regt. in the night sub sector of the front line. Lt. Colonel R.H.T. SYMONDS-TAYLER, 15th Bn HEREFORDSHIRE Regt. attached to Bn. for instructional purposes.	
MAROC	5		Enemy's attitude quiet on all fronts. His aim at starting minor patrol was fairly active, our Scouts and our artillery Lewis gunning and machine gun activity Quiet. 1 W.O. wounded round TRIANGLE. 9 O.R. wounded.	aca?
	8/9/10		At 4.20 p.m. a raiding party, which had been preparing in LES BREBIS crossed No Mans land under cover of a Smoke barrage and entered the enemy trenches on both sides of the apex of the TRIANGLE capturing 9 Germans and inflicting considerable losses on the enemy. Several dug outs were bombed. Our party returned under cover of a heavy artillery barrage. A handwritten message from HARRISON had previously been sent attracting the enemy attention.	aca? aca?

WAR DIARY
or
INTELLIGENCE SUMMARY

Army Form C. 2118.

Place	Date	Hour	Summary of Events and Information	Remarks and references to Appendices
MAROC	11		Assistance was given of one of our aeroplanes which was low over the trenches and was subjected to the fire thereby disorganising the getting of the M.G. fire thereby. Our casualties — 2nd Lt P. HEMING wounded. 1 O.R. wounded. 2 O.R. missing. 1 O.R. killed.	Details and correspondence attached to diary see copy.
	12		Lt Colonel R.H.T SYMONDS-TAYLER returns to his own unit. Capt H.C. HEYS-THOMSON and Lieut A.B. HODGE join the Bn.	
	13		Bn. relieved by the 7th Northants Regt. and became Bde in Brigade Support.	
	14		Canadian raid carried out a very successful raid on the enemy's lines B of the Southern Crassier.	
	15		2nd Lt P. joined Bn. 2 O.R. wounded. Work consisted always routine of carrying and digging parties.	
	16			
	17		Bn. relieves the 7th Northants Regt. in the front line. Major D. CAMPBELL 8th Bn A. & S. Highlanders attached to the Bn.	
	18		2nd Lieut H. de COURCY killed by an aerial dart.	

WAR DIARY or INTELLIGENCE SUMMARY

Army Form C. 2118.

Place	Date	Hour	Summary of Events and Information	Remarks and references to Appendices
MAROC	March 19		Usual hostile bomb bombardment on our wire opposite KING STREET. Retaliation frequent, called for and extra precaution taken. By Corp. DELANEY and 2 O.R. wounded. A successful enterprising patrol was congratulated on it by the G.O.C.	Report congratulating them on attack
	20		No 9817 Corp. C. McDERMOTT No 9432 Corp. McNAMARA, and No 9136 Pte. W. ENGLISH No 7904 Pte. P. O'LEARY receiving the Military medal for daring during an air raid of the 10th. No 253 Pte. MAHONEY mentioned in 1st Army Routine Order No 589, for an act of courage i.e. giving some of his blood to a wounded officer from Sutt being wounded. (Smith recorded on in Regt. Conduct Sheet.) 4 O.R. join ed B/n 3 O.R. wounded.	enacted
	21 22		Lieut A.T. JENNING and 2nd Lieut H.C. OULTON joined Bn. 1 OR killed 1 OR wounded. Usual hostile bombing. Bn relieved by the 7th Northants Regt. and became Bn in Divisional Reserve.	
LES BREBIS	23 24		Training and platoon drill 2nd Lieut H.W. OSBORNE joins Bn. 2 O.R. killed	enacted

Army Form C. 2118.

WAR DIARY or INTELLIGENCE SUMMARY
(Erase heading not required.)

Place	Date	Hour	Summary of Events and Information	Remarks and references to Appendices
MAROC	25		Capt T.G. SAUNDERS 2nd Lieut J.J. KELLY 2nd Lieut C.D. SMYTH join Bn. 17 Officers 105 K.O.Y.L.I. is Strength on march etc:	
	26/27		Training and platoon drill. Operation order received to be relieved by the 9th K.O.Y.L.I. and march to rest camp. This order was subsequently cancelled.	
	28/29		Training. Platoon drill.	
	30		The Batt. relieved the 7th Northamptons in Reg. in the night of 1 OR killed & 1 OR wounded. Quiet day, except an occasional display of enemy. Our artillery replied with good effect. Ratification on Corps routine orders. 2nd Lt. P.C. Hitchcock. 2nd Lt. W.D. Laude. 2nd Lt. R.A.A. Karrach awarded the M.C.	
	31.		Ratn. The following Officers W.O.'s & N.C.O.'s when inclusion in despatches in London Gazette dated 4-1-17. Lt Col Murphy 4.O.M.C. 2nd Lt. Tank Capt H.B. Matheson 6877 R.Q.M.S. A Vieley 7858 Sgt (acting R.R.M.S.) W.H. Dowd 8876 Sgt A. Nibills.	

A.J. Murphy Lt Col
2nd Comd Bn R.Ir. Regt.

"A" Form. Army Form C. 2121.
MESSAGES AND SIGNALS. No. of Message............

Prefix	Code	Words	Charge	This message is on a/c of:	Recd. at .... m.
Office of Origin and Service Instructions.					Date 20/1/17
BH6	Sent At ... m. To ... By ...			.... Service. (Signature of "Franking Officer.")	From BH6 By Pte Whitlock

TO { BH2 (FOOTBALL)   W.P.

Sender's Number	Day of Month	In reply to Number	AAA
BM386	20		

Message from Brady begins aaa
G.O.C. is exceedingly pleased
to hear of excellent patrol
carried out last night aaa
Ends aaa

(19)

From	BH6 (FOXWELL)
Place	
Time	9 PM

The above may be forwarded as now corrected. (Z)

Censor.   Signature of Addressee or person authorised to telegraph in his name.

* This line should be erased if not required.

Army Form C. 2118.

WAR DIARY
or
INTELLIGENCE SUMMARY.
(Erase heading not required.)

Vol 31

Place	Date	Hour	Summary of Events and Information	Remarks and references to Appendices
[continued]			1st Battalion the Leinster Regiment. War Diary for the month of February 1914.	

WAR DIARY
or
INTELLIGENCE SUMMARY.

Army Form C. 2118.

Place	Date	Hour	Summary of Events and Information	Remarks and references to Appendices
MAROC	1-8-17		Trenches quiet day. Hostile aerial dart & minenwerfer in the evening. Our retaliation effective. Capt Bolsover killed & 1 O.R. wounded.	
"	2		Petition 1st Capt Strong killed & 2 O.R. wounded	T.P.
"	3		Relieved by the 7th Loyal N. Lancs Regt. Relief completed 10.30 am. A.B.C. Coys in Villemarie	T.P.
"	4		Relieved the 9th R. Sussex Regt. in support A.B.C. Coys in Villemarie	T.P.
"	5		D Coy in O.G.1. & Hugo.	T.P.
"	6		Bn. moved Bombing test "	T.P.
"	7		C Coy relieved D Coy in O.G.1 & the keeps about 9pm. Major Ford & Major Holmes (Clifton) Stowaphen Lane.	T.P.
"	8		Bn. reserve. Party of officers from 11th R. Warwicks came to reconnoitre our front line. 2nd Lt Glenn recd O Oder. (No 98 regarding 2nd Lt M.J. Callen A Coy and 2nd Lt J.H Smyth & 2nd L CO. Strumferrots arrived)	T.P. Mr Lythe
"	9		Bn. reserve working parties	T.P.
	10		"	

Army Form C. 2118.

WAR DIARY
or
INTELLIGENCE SUMMARY.
(Erase heading not required.)

Instructions regarding War Diaries and Intelligence Summaries are contained in F. S. Regs., Part II. and the Staff Manual respectively. Title pages will be prepared in manuscript.

Place	Date	Hour	Summary of Events and Information	Remarks and references to Appendices
MAROC	11.		Relieved by the 11th Warwicks, about 4 pm the relief completed the Battn. marched by platoons to NOEUX-LES-MINES, where we billeted for the night. The last platoon arrived about 9-30 pm. J.B.Coy.	
NOEUX-LES-MINES	12.		The Battn. left NOEUX-LES-MINES at 10-5 & marched to FOUQUEREUIL. The Field Cashier commanded in Chief inspected the Bn. during the march on Route. (about 200 yds east of VAUDRICOURT) & saw my Bnd. with the offrs. & men [of] the march past the Battn. He arrived at FOUQUEREUIL at 1pm Battn. in billets to have equipment, clothing etc examined by O.C. Bns. unites the Battn. in billets.	J.P. J.P. Copy attached highlighted
FOUQUEREUIL	13.		Billets	
	14.		"	J.P.
	15.		"	
	16.		Practice parade for the French Corps in Chief (& the C.O.) at 11-30 am.	J.P.
	17.		The Battn. paraded at 8-45 am to march to HESDIGNEUL for inspection (with the 8th R.F.) under Col. A.D. MURPHY, M.C. General Rivelle Comr in Chief of the French Army inspected us about 10-40 am	J.P. Remarks of the J.P. General attached copy
	18.		Divine service parade.	

2353 Wt. W2544/1454 700,000 5/15 D.D. & L. A.D.S.S. Forms/C. 2118.

Army Form C. 2118.

WAR DIARY
or
INTELLIGENCE SUMMARY.
(Erase heading not required.)

Instructions regarding War Diaries and Intelligence Summaries are contained in F. S. Regs., Part II. and the Staff Manual respectively. Title pages will be prepared in manuscript.

Place	Date	Hour	Summary of Events and Information	Remarks and references to Appendices
	Feb.			
FOUQUEREUIL	19.		Training 8.00 am to 12-00 pm & 2 pm to 4.30 pm Platoon & Section training	J.P.
	20.		Specialists under specialists N.C.O.	
	21.		Battalion route march about 4 miles.	
	22.		Training 8-30 am to 12-30 pm & 2 pm to 4.30 pm.	J.P.
	23.		Bde Exercise C.O. (Hughes) and 2 Company Offr & all officers attended	Returning J.P. Appendix
	24.		Training 8-30 to 12-30 pm	J.P.
	25.		Church Parade	J.P.
	26.		Training 8-30 am to 12-30 pm extension of Recon P.O. to rear	No attack exercise.
	27.		" "	J.P.
	28.		Training 8-30 am to 11-30am Batt: attack & 2pm to 4-30 pm to fire	J.P.

A.J. Murphy Lt Col.
Comdg 2ND Kents Rgt.

2353 Wt. W2544/1454 700,000 5/15 D. D. & L. A.D.S.S. Forms/C. 2118.

Army Form C. 2118.

WAR DIARY
or
INTELLIGENCE SUMMARY.
(Erase heading not required.)

Vol 32

War Diary for the month of
March 1919
of
1st Battalion the Servian Regiment.

WAR DIARY or INTELLIGENCE SUMMARY

Army Form C. 2118.

Place	Date	Hour	Summary of Events and Information	Remarks and references to Appendices
FOUQUEREUIL	March 1.		Marched from Fouquereuil about 8-30 am to Hallicourt arrived there at 11-30 am & billeted there.	
HALLICOURT	2.		Billets. 2nd Lt W.J. Richar[d]s 2nd Lt J. Scott & Lt R.J.L. Hesketh-Jones joined Battn.	
"	3.		At 9-15 am the B.O. Off. & 6 Lt. corporals proceeded to reconnoitre the Souchez sector. At 9-30 am the Battn. took the command of 2 Coy R. French for Bn. H.Q.	
"			Marched to Bouvigny Huts, arriving at 1 pm, the Batts 8th Worcesters reached the Canadian Baths. The relief was completed at 10 pm	
ABLAIN ST NAZAIRE	4.		Bn. hqrs (the Lorette defences) near Ablain St Nazaire & relieved B Co. in the Canadian Baths. The relief was completed at noon.	
"			Bn. Hqrs. at 7 pm the Batt. was relieved by 1st Batt. 2 R. Berks Reg. & moved to the R.H. salient. Relieving & relieved the 1st Canadian Battn. The relief was completed at 10-30 pm	
SOUCHEZ	5-6.		Trenches. The usual trench duties carried out. Also 1 officer & 7 men sick to hospital.	
"			Trenches. 1st[?] & 2nd killed.	
"	5.		Trenches. Brigade 5 Day. 10 R. killed. 2nd Lt A.E. Phillips joined from hospital.	
"	7.		At 2 O R.M. the Bn. was relieved by 1st Batt. Irish Rif. & marched back to the Bouvigny Huts	

Army Form C. 2118.

WAR DIARY
or
INTELLIGENCE SUMMARY.
(Erase heading not required.)

Instructions regarding War Diaries and Intelligence Summaries are contained in F. S. Regs., Part II. and the Staff Manual respectively. Title pages will be prepared in manuscript.

Place	Date	Hour	Summary of Events and Information	Remarks and references to Appendices
Sailly	7.		Batt. transport moved from Hersin & Vaim En Gohelle	S.P.
"	8.		Funeral, field day	S.P.
"	9.		Lt G. Rexford R.A.M.C. joined from base	S.P.
"	10		Between 10 am & 10-30 am the enemy bombarded our trenches with H.T.M & Whig. Bombs. During the bomb[ar]dment the firing line of A & C Coys. Batt. Res & our heavy Artillery retaliated. The Batt. was relieved by the 2nd Bn. Leinsters during the night 10/11th about 1am. 2nd Lt A. G. Plaskitt got wounded & Lt 10 O.R. killed & 7 O.R. wounded during relief.	S.P.
"	11		Inspected billets 3 am at Vaim-En-Gohelle Lt Col LL L'Glad Maud(?) transferred sen. Major R	S.P.
Vaim En Gohelle	12		Bath 8-30 am Shg 12-30 pm Musketry. General Chaw off. B.P. Ch.	S.P.
"	13		Coy training from 8-30 am to 12-30 pm	S.P.
"	14		" " " "	S.P.
"	15		The Batt. celebrated St Patrick's day. Elect. Prints at Mass. R. C. Chapel, Vaim-En-Gohelle 9.10 o'clock rosée to rare mass carried out S.E. Church parade. Capt W.M. Dickie R.A.M.C. in lieu of Lt J. Rexford	S.P.

2353 Wt. W2544/1454 700,000 5/15 D. D. & L. A.D.S.S.-Forms/C. 2118.

WAR DIARY or INTELLIGENCE SUMMARY

Army Form C. 2118.

Place	Date	Hour	Summary of Events and Information	Remarks and references to Appendices
SAINS-EN- GOHELLE	16.		1 Officer & 54 OR proceed to the 24th Div. camp school ALLOUAGNE.	A.P.
			LT. M.A. Higgins & 50 OR joined the Batt. H.Q. arrived at 6.15 p.m. to relieve the 7th hostels in front line. Relief was not done. The relief was completed at 11.5 p.m.	
Bouchez	17.		6.20 a.m. the Batt. ordered to the front line for Batt. interlude. Between 8-9 p.m. the enemy again at L.M.G. and rifle Artillery retal. 1 OR killed 10 R wounded	A.P.
	18.		Quiet day a little sniping. Between 8-9 p.m. some excitement. 1 OR killed. 10 R wounded and L.V. Heathington Batt. to hospital. 2 & OR wounded	A.P.
	19.		At 5.10 a.m. enemy raid our post in Elephant lane, killing one OR & wounding 5 OR. The 12 Bde. are taken prisoner & escaped from the enemy. of 147 wounded. At 6.5 p.m. the hostile bomb[?] to retire from the post back to the by post showing the raid. The enemy search 25 minutes after. Two OR wounded during the evening	A.P.
	20.		Two OR wounded at 7.30 a.m. by sniper. Between 11 a.m. & 12.30 p.m. our Battery bombarded the enemy line at L[?] of intensity of 2 min.	A.P.

Army Form C. 2118.

WAR DIARY
or
INTELLIGENCE SUMMARY.
(Erase heading not required.)

Instructions regarding War Diaries and Intelligence Summaries are contained in F.S. Regs., Part II. and the Staff Manual respectively. Title pages will be prepared in manuscript.

Place	Date	Hour	Summary of Events and Information	Remarks and references to Appendices
Souchez	March 21		Trenches. Quiet day. 2/O L/C Baker wounded 4 p.m. At 5 p.m. our heavy Artillery bombarded the enemy from the line for 30 minutes. The enemy did not reply. 1 O.R. killed.	A.P.
"	22		Quiet day. 2 O.R. wounded.	A.P.
"	23		Relieved by 7th Lonsdales L.R.E. commencing at 8 p.m. Relief complete 10 p.m. Batt'n in reserve from the reserve. Lorette Defences.	A.P.
"	24		Btl in reserve. 1 O.R. wounded.	A.P.
"	25		" Evening 2 L/C wounded. 2 O.R. joined Batt'n.	A.P.
"	26		" Sniper Barnes at 9-30 & 10-30 am.	A.P.
"	27		" O.C. visits the Batt'n.	A.P.
"	28		" Lt Col A.D. Murphy M.C. returned off leave.	A.P.
"	29		Btl in reserve.	
"	30		Btl in reserve. Relieved by the 86th Canadian Batt'n 10-30 p.m. & proceeded to the billets shot Bichers on leaving the 2nd Trench the Supported Line.	
"	31		Rest day. Coy/ parade 12-15 am. Quiet day.	A.P.

A.D. Murphy Lt. Col.
Comdg 2/10 Man. & Rent.

2nd BATTN. LEINSTER REGIMENT

73rd INFANTRY BRIGADE

24th DIVISION

APRIL 1917

WAR DIARY

INTELLIGENCE SUMMARY

2nd Leinster Regiment
for the month of
April 1917

WAR DIARY
or
INTELLIGENCE SUMMARY.
(Erase heading not required.)

Army Form C. 2118.

Place	Date	Hour	Summary of Events and Information	Remarks and references to Appendices
Cuinchy	MARCH 31	10-30	Hazy. Enemy blowing out front line. Vicinity of Left Coy HQ & Coy Front.	J.P.
"	APRIL 1		Lt M.A. Higgins killed. Quiet day. Casualties reported during forenoon 2/Lt MOLT. W.E.G. Rickett killed. 2 OR killed & 18 OR wounded.	J.P.
"	2		Quiet. No movement visible of the enemy on the front line. Enemy shelling our front line at 10-30pm moderately with Battery in our front line. The EO ordered Stand at 10-40pm. The Battn stood down 11-30pm. Casualties 6 OR wounded. Went to Bowly in 3 hospital.	J.P.
"	3		Our artillery very active. Rifle & front line & enemy and not heard at 12-45am the Patrols returned 2am. No enemy encountered. 6 OR killed.	J.P.
"	4		Our artillery very active. Battn relieved by 7th London & Regt commencing of relief completed 12-30am. Lt Bates wounded & Lt Willis at 3pm 10 Capt F.G. Coombs to hospital. 2 OR wounded	J.P.
"	5			
"	6		Battle Zone 10. Practice Battle Attack.	J.P.
"	7			

WAR DIARY or INTELLIGENCE SUMMARY

Army Form C. 2118.

Place	Date	Hour	Summary of Events and Information	Remarks and references to Appendices
	APRIL			
FOUILLE 10	8	9.30pm	Divs. orders Practice attack. The G.O.C. 2d Division addressed the Battn.	S.P.
"	9		1 O.R. killed in AIX NOULETTE. 2nd Lt. H. Crowe from hospital. Battn. the Battn. orders to proceed to trenches at 6-10 pm to take part in an attack on the BOIS-EN-HACHE. Casualties 2 O.R. 1 O.R.	S.P.
"	10		Billets. Carrying out the arrangements. 1 O.R. slightly wounded at AIX NOULETTE	S.P.
SOUCHEZ	11		Billets. At 9 p.m. the Battn. proceeded to occupy trenches in our own front line between Northumberland Post & Pattern Row Post 5. Relieved the 7th Northamptonshire Regt. Dummy relief ourselves relieved the 4 Trench Mortar Bt.	S.P.
"	12	3 am	Battn. in position in occupied trenches.	S.P.
"	"	4 am	Casualty 1 O.R. commenced assembling in NO-MANS-LAND.	
"	"	5 am (Zero hour)	The corporation with the attacks on Vimy Ridge & the Battn. attacked the BOIS-EN-HACHE Ridge in co-operation with the 9th Royal Sussex Regt.	Narrative attached S.P.
"	"	5-9 am	Reported to Bde that Battn. had advanced under barrage	
"	"	6.10 am	Reported to Bde that 1st Objective had been captured & was being consolidated. Other parties had reached German 2nd & 3rd objective line. Enemy M.G. S.O.S. of the line very heavy.	S.P.

Army Form C. 2118.

WAR DIARY
or
INTELLIGENCE SUMMARY.

(Erase heading not required.)

Instructions regarding War Diaries and Intelligence Summaries are contained in F. S. Regs., Part II. and the Staff Manual respectively. Title pages will be prepared in manuscript.

Place	Date	Hour	Summary of Events and Information	Remarks and references to Appendices
SOUCHEZ	12	5-7 am	Relief as reported as follows. Holding the front line about Vol. 2.4. Consisted of 2 and relating Each Batt 2 hours of fire line with 2 Batt in supports in the right (2-3 Batt myself ? an 4 line) A trench with reserve on the left they find lent. Every expire from the direction of Bois de GIVENCHY reported to be neighbourhood of casualties. In Feb. MG were active from this neighbourhood.	J.P.
"	"	5-6 am	M.G. Detachment ordered to proceed with Vickers guns to stop of front line. Connected J.J. 129 by R.E. (Supplent Co). D.B. sent time orders to push derived task and reported the new Knivets available at dark or stop formed on the line sufp.	J.P.
"	"	9 am		J.P.
"	"	noon	Situation unchanged received sketch	J.P.
"	"	3-10 pm		
"	"	10-4 pm		
"	13th	4-5-30 pm	Situation quiet, our artillery not engaged	
"	"	3-30 pm	Officers taken out and out to ascertain situation on right flank. Reports a nothing too very and it may use the ground to the left in dry out Jo	
"	"	4 pm	Recon information that Bde had newly occupied GIVENCHY & part of the	

WAR DIARY or INTELLIGENCE SUMMARY

Army Form C. 2118.

Place	Date	Hour	Summary of Events and Information	Remarks and references to Appendices
Sauchez	13	6.55 p.m.	Recvd Sy (Bdy) order 6of8 After arrangd w arty to put Bn into attack w/ Establish posts in 2 NOD the line of Enemy trenches - now reported to be just on the left of the 10th Canadian Bde on the right & the 9th Royal Scots on the left	J.P.
"	"	7.30 p.m.	Heavy trench mortar on the eastern side of road Report time of attack with Bn Batn in the life & right	J.P.
"	"	7.40 p.m.	Bath HQ established in offical permanent line about 1½F 26-70.	J.P.
"	"	7.52 p.m.	Reported to Bde the batt lodging line in water only 2-3 yrs between Cité-de-Calonne & ANGRES with people & asmn the posn	J.P.
"	14	7 a.m.	Bn relvd by 12th Rl Royal Fusiliers & Bombed to Billets in Force 10/ Rear Posns - in GOSELLE.	J.P.
Fosse 10	15		Billets. Bde calls a checking of casualties after the action	J.P.
"	16	11 a.m.	Billets. G.O.C. 24th Div. Genvd. Holbrook Oaks, & congratulated them on their good work in the attack.	
"	17		Billets.	
"	18	2.30 p.m.	Proceed to VE HILARE District. Bon HVy in HOUCHIN. Arrived at BOUCHIN 6 p.m. & remained one night.	

Army Form C. 2118.

WAR DIARY
or
INTELLIGENCE SUMMARY.
(Erase heading not required.)

Instructions regarding War Diaries and Intelligence Summaries are contained in F.S. Regs., Part II. and the Staff Manual respectively. Title pages will be prepared in manuscript.

Place	Date	Hour	Summary of Events and Information	Remarks and references to Appendices
HOUDLIN	19	10.10am	Batts left Hoodin & continued march to rest area. Arrived AUCHEL about 5pm.	A.P.
AUCHEL	20	9.45am	Marched to LAIRES & arrived in LAIRES about 12.30pm. Batts billeted here for rest.	A.P.
LAIRES	21		Billets.	
"	22		Billets.	
"	23		From 9.30 to 12.30pm Training of Specialists & Platoon training.	A.P.
"	24		Billets. At 11am B.C. 73rd Bde. inspected the Batts. J. about 12 noon.	
"	25		Billets. Training from 9am to 12.30pm.	
"	26		~4.30pm. Bn. received orders to be ready to move to NOEUX-LES-MINES area. 11.30am Bn. ordered to be ready to move at 1pm. 1.20pm ordered to be at BOURN Rd P327 (entry point) at 2.15pm. The Batts marched to HOUCHIN & arrived about 5.10pm.	A.P.
HOUCHIN	27	9.10am	Batts marched to HOUCHIN arrived 12.30pm. Batts encamped here.	A.P.
HOUCHIN	28		Batts in Camp.	
"	29		" " Divine Service by R.C. in Village Church at 9am.	A.P.

Place	Date	Hour	Summary of Events and Information	Remarks and references to Appendices
Howitzer	29	11 am	Left Service on football ground at 11am. W/s & guns at 11am to camp. Batt. in camp. Enemy S. room to 12.20 pm & 2 pm to 3 pm	
	30		2nd casualties during the month ending 30th April 1917. 5 officers killed 37 O.R. 7 officers wounded & 182 O.R. 3 O.R. missing	

A J Murphy Lt Col
Comdg 210 Kimberley Regt

Narrative of Operations of 2nd Bn. The Leinster Regiment from 9 p.m. 11th April 1917 to 10 a.m. 14th April 1917

11th April

1. **Preliminary.** A short final practice was held in the morning and final instructions issued to Company Commanders during the afternoon. In the late afternoon it was notified that "Zero Hour" would be at 5 a.m. instead of at 2 a.m. as first arranged. Wet afternoon with heavy snow in the evening.

2. **Initial Movements.** Between 9 p.m. and 11.30 p.m. Platoons left billets at FOSSE 10. (near PETIT SAINS) and moved in fighting kit via AIX NOULETTE and main ARRAS Road to our old trenches in SOUCHEZ Section. Snowing ceased and prospects of a fine night. As Platoons arrived at HEADQUARTER TRENCH they were provided with tea and a small rum issue and were given extra equipment such as bombs, tools, wire-cutters, etc, according to the scale previously arranged.

12th April.

Last Platoon arrived about 2 a.m.

Detachments from 129th Co. R.E. and 73rd M.G. Company were attached to Platoons en-route and moved with them to front trenches. Detachment from 12th Sherwood Foresters (Pioneers) arrived about 2.30 a.m.

Enemy's attitude very quiet and there was only slight shelling in the vicinity of ARRAS Road.

3. **ASSEMBLY**

Assembly commenced at 4 a.m. (ZERO - 1). Snow now again falling heavily and trenches and ground in a terrible state. Our first wave deployed outside our wire and second wave in front of our parapets. Reserve Company in TUNNEL. A few casualties from machine-gun and rifle fire which became fairly brisk shortly before zero hour. At 4.31 a.m. reported Battalion in Assembly Positions and ready to advance.

4. **ASSAULT**

At 5 a.m. (ZERO Hour) the two waves (3 Companies) advanced under our barrage. A blinding snow-storm still blowing and weather bitterly cold. The state of the ground made movement almost impossible and progress was extremely slow. NO MAN'S LAND, a series of craters and shell holes filled with water and edged with soft mud in places two or three feet deep.

Enemy immediately opened heavy rifle and machine-gun fire on our advancing lines, firing apparently from his front line and from natural cover between the two objectives. The right Company was badly enfiladed across the SOUCHEZ Valley from the direction of BOIS DE GIVENCHY and suffered severely.

Hostile barrage was feeble and enemy contented himself with a few 4.2 cm. and 5.9 cm. in rear of KELLET line and on HELMER and HEADQUARTER TRENCHES.

Our barrage appeared very good though we had several casualties from our own shell.

5. **FIRST OBJECTIVE**

At 5.10 a.m. our barrage lifted and our men captured the German front line which was in very bad condition and only occupied at certain localities. The hostile wire had been well destroyed and no trouble was experienced in crossing it. A few prisoners were taken and the remaining Germans got away backwards towards their support line.

The survivors of our first wave pushed across the front trench and went on under our barrage to the second objective (150 - 250x).

6. **SECOND OBJECTIVE**

The state of the ground in rear of the enemy's front line was even worse than the OLD NO MAN'S LAND and the men found tremendous difficulty in advancing. Hostile rifle and machine-gun fire was still intense and casualties were heavy, particular damage being caused by the destructive enfilade fire from the Valley. All Officers with first wave were either killed or wounded and very few leaders survived. Nevertheless, a few men succeeded in reaching the second objective on both flanks, and found the trench almost obliterated but the enemy were resisting strongly from natural cover in vicinity. Bomb encounters and hand to hand fighting took place and there were several casualties on both sides. At two points our men remained in possession and grouped themselves into small parties. Many individual acts of gallantry were performed at this stage.

7. THE DEFENSIVE FLANK

The Platoon detailed to form the defensive flank on the right of the attack suffered heavy casualties from rifle and machine-gun fire from across the SOUCHEZ Valley and from the trenches in rear of LONG SAP.

After the intense bombardment of the previous week, it was most difficult to recognise the embankment which was the objective of this platoon, and a number of the men seem to have outrun their objective and assaulted LONG SAP and the trench in rear of it which was in good condition and strongly held. A stiff fight at close quarters took place here and several Germans were killed. In spite of severe losses, our men established a post at this point. Corporal Cunningham, armed with a Lewis gun and a few bombs accounted for at least 20 of the enemy, and although wounded in four places held the post almost single handed until his ammunition and bombs were exhausted. The few survivors of the Platoon, made their way back to the embankment and were deployed on the right flank facing South and so kept touch between our old line and the right flank of the captured front line.

8. COUNTER-ATTACKS

The only serious counter-attacks made by the enemy were directed against our right flank and were made from the good trenches in the valley below and behind LONG SAP.

The first of these (about 40 men) was made against the post in the vicinity of the second objective established by the Right Company. For about three quarter of an hour this post under Lieut E.J. MAGNER held out and caused many casualties to the enemy. When ammunition and bombs ran out the survivors withdrew to the German Front line and were re-organised in the line of Resistance.

The second counter-attack (about 20 men) was repulsed by Corporal Cunningham's post near LONG SAP, but this post had ultimately to withdraw owing to want of ammunition and bombs.

9. SITUATION at 7.30 am.

Battalion holding the enemy's front line in touch with 9th Bn Royal Sussex in this line on our left and in touch with our old front line. Advanced posts withdrawn from second objective (with exception of small post on our left which remained lying out until dusk) and established about 40 yards in front of our new line of Resistance (i.e. enemy's front line). Consolidation of German front line proceeding. Pioneers working at Communication trench to connect captured line to our old line. Gap between two Companies filled by two Sections from Reserve Company. Enemy's rifle and machine-gun fire still heavy especially from the right.

10. CONSOLIDATION

Consolidation was very difficult owing to the mud and water and to the battered state of the captured trenches. By 9am, two Platoons of the Reserve Company as well as the R.E. Detachment and the survivors of Assaulting Companies were employed on consolidation of three strong points in enemy's line. Fair progress made with these by 12 noon. The work of Pioneers on Cme Trench enfiladed by hostile shelling and party was withdrawn at 9.30am.

11. SITUATION at 11.30 am.

Enemy rifle and machine-gun fire practically ceased and no signs of Infantry activity reported. Hostile artillery shelling KELLET line and HEADQUARTER TRENCH.

12. EVACUATION OF WOUNDED

At 12.5 pm, stretcher parties were ordered out and searched NOMANS LAND and vicinity of captured German line for wounded: carrying of stretchers extremely difficult owing to the state of ground. No opposition shown by the eny.

(3)

13. ESTIMATED CASUALTIES
12.30 pm. Reported estimated casualties 10 Officers and 150 other ranks. Asked for reinforcements before night.

14. ENEMY'S ATTITUDE
During the afternoon and evening the enemy showed no further activity. Desultory shelling of our old support lines continued all day.

15. EXTENSION OF RIGHT FLANK
In order to obtain better observation towards the valley and so greater security, it was decided to advance our right flank tonight to the South-eastern edge of wood. This move was to be carried out by a Platoon of the Reserve Company soon after dark, but the operation was postponed on receipt of information from Brigade H.Q about 9 pm. that a further attack on the enemy trenches on our right just North of Souchez River would be carried out tonight by 7th Bn Northamptonshire Regt.

Decided to carry out this advance of our right in conjunction with attack by 7th Northamptons but the latter was cancelled by fresh instructions received at 11. pm.

13th April.
The move to new position which was attempted by two sections of the Reserve Company soon after 3.am. was unsuccessful owing to the darkness of the night and the vigilance of the enemy and it was decided to postpone the operation until daylight, when direction was more simple and when the enemy was less watchful.

After daylight the movement was successfully carried out without molestation and a new strong point which over looked the river, and the hostile trenches astride of it was consolidated. There were no signs of enemy occupation by day of these trenches.

16. PROGRESS OF WORK
Work progressed well on four new strong points and a good deal of wiring was done. Except for desultory shelling and a little long range sniping enemy did not attempt to hinder work. Stretcher parties collected many dead and were assisted by bearers from Field Ambulance line. A duckboard path to connect captured line with our old front was completed.

17. PATROLS
Patrols sent out during afternoon reported no signs of enemy in his original second line and many indications there of a hurried retreat. Enemy second line in valley in good condition and a considerable amount of equipment and rations etc. about. One prisoner captured in dugout there by Lieut W.J. PORTER. Several German and some of our own dead found in the vicinity of LONGSAP.

18. THE ENEMY WITHDRAWS
Besides the patrol reports there were other indications towards the evening that the enemy had withdrawn from his trenches on the Eastern slopes of the BOIS-EN-HACHE. At about 5.30 pm, information was received that a patrol of the 9th Royal Sussex had entered ANGRES. The Battalion was ordered to move forward and establish a line of posts, along the SOUCHEZ River between CITE DU GRUMONT and ANGRES.

At about 6.15 pm, "D" Company under Captain M. ALGEO. moved forward in artillery formation and reached the line of SOUCHEZ River without opposition. Here an outpost line was established and touch was gained with the 9th Royal Sussex Regt. on the left and the 10th Canadian Brigade on the right. Patrols pushed across the river reported the ridge East of river clear of enemy.

Fires observed in LENS and LIEVIN. A small party of enemy seen near FOSSE 6 retired eastwards.

19. RELIEF

At about 4.30am, the leading companies of 12th Royal Fusiliers arrived at Advanced Battalion H.Q. to relieve Battalion. Owing to darkness and state of ground, the relief of "A" company was postponed till daylight. Relief of Battalion was completed about 7.30 a.m. and Companies marched back to FOSSE 10 across country to HOULETTE WOOD and down main ARRAS–BETHUNE Road.

20. CASUALTIES

Killed

Officers

Captain	W. P. Liston	5th Bn Leinster Regt
Captain	J. J. Kelly	7th Bn Leinster Regt
2/Lieut	J. H. Smyth	5th Bn Leinster Regt
"	H. S. Oulton	4th Bn Leinster Regt

Other Ranks – 48.

Wounded

Officers

Lieut	P. P. McCann M.C.	4th Bn Leinster Regt
"	E. J. Wagner	3rd Bn Leinster Regt
"	R. G. L. Stirling	Leinster Regt
"	H. J. Cullen	5th Bn Leinster Regt
2/Lieut	J. Quinlan	Leinster Regt
"	C. Eastwood	Leinster Regt

Other Ranks – 155.

Missing

Officers – Nil

Other Ranks – 3

Total Casualties – 10 Officers 206 Other Ranks.

A. D. Murphy – Lt Colonel
Commanding 2nd Bn Leinster Regt

Preliminary Instructions
Memorandum No. 1
War Diary

Medical Arrangements

A Battalion Collecting Station will be established in the SUNKEN ROAD in rear of No 8 Post (about S.2.b 05.20)

The Battalion Stretcher-bearers under Captain W.M. Bacon. R.A.M.C. will be assembled at this point as soon after ZERO hour as the hostile barrage permits. From this Collecting Station stretcher parties will go out and will search NO MAN'S LAND and the vicinity of the enemy's front line for serious cases which will be carried back to the Collecting Station. Relays of bearers from 74th Field Ambulance will evacuate the stretcher cases from the Battalion Collecting Station, moving via COMPANY TRENCH and so to the main ARRAS ROAD.

All walking wounded will be directed to the Northamptonshire Regiment Aid Post in HEADQUARTER TRENCH via COMPANY TRENCH. Walking wounded are to bring in their arms and equipment.

Stretcher cases in the enemy second line or between the enemy front and second line will be evacuated before dawn, if possible, by returning carrying parties or by parties withdrawing to our lines before daylight. Such parties will be ordered to search for wounded when coming back.

In no case will any of the men detailed for the Assault, for Mopping-up or for consolidation return to our lines for the purpose of conducting wounded unless definitely ordered to do so by an Officer. All ranks will be warned of this order.

Prisoners

Prisoners captured in the enemy's first or second line will be collected into batches in the trench in which they are taken and sent back as time permits under small escorts which should not exceed 10%. Men are to be warned that they are not allowed to leave the captured trenches to escort prisoners unless specially detailed for this duty by an Officer or senior N.C.O.

A collecting post for prisoners will be established on the SUNKEN ROAD in rear of No 7 Post (about S.2.b.20.15). No man of the Battalion will escort prisoners beyond this point.

Non-Commissioned Officers

Each Company will leave behind at the Transport Lines, under the R.S.M. at least 1 Sergt, 1 Corporal and 1 Lance-Corporal. These N.C.Os will be utilised, if necessary, to replace casualties in the platoons and must be carefully selected. In the above numbers the N.C.Os at present attending the class under the R.S.M and the Company Instructors at ALLOUAGNE may be included. None of the N.C.O's class will join their companies before the attack unless specially asked for by O.C. Companies.

Dumps

Two advanced dumps of S.A.A, Mills Bombs, Smoke Bombs, Rifle Grenades, Very Lights, Shovels, Wiring Material, Sandbags, etc, will be formed, one at ROTTEN ROW POST and one at NORTHUMBERLAND POST. O.C. "D" Coy will detail a man to take charge of each of the above dumps, under the supervision of the Coy Sergt Major of "D" Coy.

A further supply of all stores will be carried forward by the reserve platoons of each assembling Company (A+B) and by the Support Company (C Coy).

Dumps of these stores will be formed

in the enemy front line trench at suitable points. The Coy. Sergt. Major of "C" Coy will be responsible for these dumps.

Lewis Guns

The fourth Lewis Gun of each Company will be kept back in Reserve in the TUNNEL in KELLET TRENCH and will be available, if required, to replace any gun damaged or put out of action. Each Company will detail 3 fully trained gunners and 3 partially trained gunners under a N.C.O to remain with this gun. These men will report to Sergt. Dixon at 6.p.m. on zero day. A reserve of magazines will be kept with these guns.

Stokes Carriers

Each Company will detail 4 men for carriers for Stokes guns. O.C. "D" Coy will detail a corporal to be in charge of this party, which will report to O.C. 7th L.T.M. Battery at an hour to be notified.

Equipment

Equipment will be as laid down on page 59 of S.S. 135 (Instructions for the Training of Divisions for Offensive Action) with the following exceptions

 (a). "A" & "B" Coys will only carry 120 rounds of S.A.A. except Reserve Platoons who carry one extra bandolier per man.

  (N.B. All bombing & Lewis Gun Sections and all N.C.Os will carry 120 rounds S.A.A. only.)

 (b). No tube helmet will be carried

 (c). No aeroplane flares will be carried.

 (d). The Assaulting Platoons of "A" & "B" Coys will not carry sandbags

2. Wirecutters at the rate of 2 per section will be carried by Assaulting Platoons and at the rate of 1 per section by Reserve Platoons and Support

(4)

Reserve Companies (A further supply of wire-cutters has been asked for)

All wire-cutters are to be tied by a lanyard to the men's shoulder-straps.

3. Assaulting Platoons carry two shovels per Section, Reserve Platoons 4 per Section. Support and Reserve Companies 4 per Section.

<u>Platoon Flags</u>

The Platoon Runner is to carry the Platoon Flag.

<u>Bombs</u>

Mills Bombs.- Each man will carry two bombs in his pockets

The equipment of Bombing and Lewis Sections and of Mopping-up Parties will be dealt with in a memorandum to be issued tomorrow

6th April 1917

(sd) B.T. Murphy. Lt Colonel
Comdg 2nd Leinster Regt

Preliminary Instructions
Memorandum No 2

Lewis Gun Equipment

Lewis Gun Equipment will be as under:—

No 1, 2, 5 & 6 Platoons (Enemy 2nd line)

Scale A

No 1.	Gun with magazine on
No 2.	One magazine carrier containing four magazines
No 3.	Spare parts.
No 4, 5, 6 & 7	Four magazines carried in packs held on back by supporting straps

Total 21 magazines

Scale B

8, 9, 10 & 11 Platoons (Enemy first line)

No 1.	Gun with magazine on
No 2.	2 magazine carriers (8 magazines)
No 3.	Spare parts
No 4, 5, 6 & 7	Two magazine carriers (32 magazines)

Total (40 magazines)

LEFT. COY Spare Equipment ROTTEN ROW.
RIGHT. COY   "   "   THUMBERLAND POST

Employment of Bombers in the Attack

The chief duties of Bombers in the Attack will be to clear trenches over which the assaulting troops have passed, to protect the flanks of the attack when it has reached and occupied the enemy's trenches, to secure enemy's communication trenches, and to form barricades so far down them that grenades cannot be thrown into the main trenches, captured by us to a bomb stop on all ways that the enemy can approach to the rifle and

(2)

must never be used to engage a target which can be dealt with more effectively with a rifle.

The following bombs will be carried by Platoons as laid down in scales named:-

Scale A

	Mills Nº 5	Rifle Grenades	Smoke Bombs
1 N.C.O	6	0	1
2 Bayonet men	6	0	2
2 Throwers	12	0	2
2 Carriers	12	0	2
2 Rifle Grenadiers	0	12	2
Total	36	12	9

Scale A will be carried by the following platoons — Nºs 1, 2, 5, 6, 13 and 14.

Scale B

	Mills Nº 5	Rifle Grenades	Smoke Bombs
1 N.C.O.	6	0	1
2 Bayonet men	8	0	2
2 Throwers	16	0	2
2 Carriers	16	0	2
2 Rifle Grenadiers	0	24	2
Total	46	24	9

Scale B will be carried by the following platoons — Nºs 3, 7, 9 and 11.

Scale C

	Mills Nº 5	Smoke Bombs	Knobkerries
1 N.C.O.	4	2	—
2 Bayonet men	2	2	1
2 Throwers	4	2	1
2 Carriers	6	2	1
2 Rifle Grenadiers	4	2	1
Total	20	10	4

Scale C to be carried by each section of Nº 18.

(3)

No 10 Platoon

Two Mills No 5 will be carried by each man in addition to the above scales laid down for each platoon.

Rifle Grenadiers will return their present rifles to the Q.M. Stores and draw Grenade rifles from Sergt Chalmers.

7th June 1917

Lt Col n
Comdg 7 Leinster Regt

PROBABLE DISPOSITION OF BATTALION
BY DAY

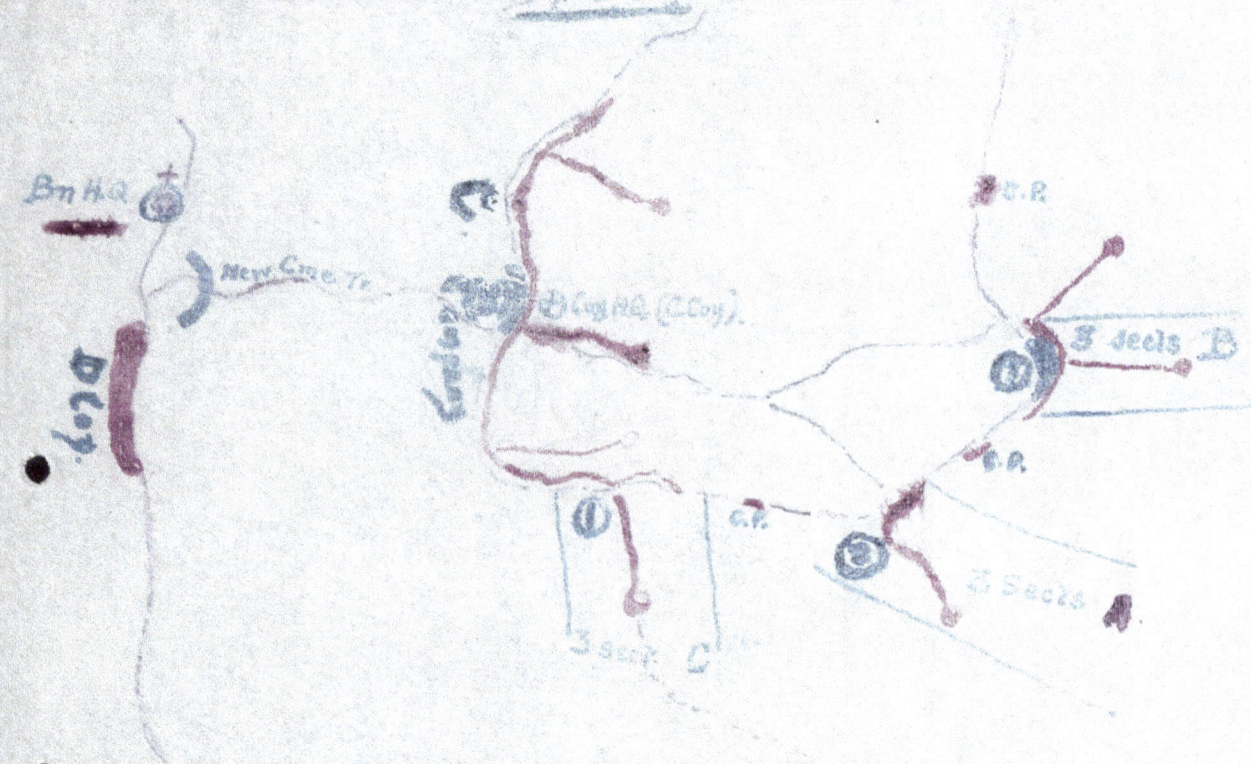

) Strong Points
● Garrisons
● C.P. Connecting Posts
▬ Advanced Posts

Preliminary Instructions
Memorandum No. 3.

After the capture of both objectives.

It will be necessary to withdraw a large proportion of the attacking troops before dawn.

The numbers and actual units to be withdrawn must depend on the general situation and the amount of opposition displayed by the enemy, and nothing definite can be laid down.

The approximate garrison to remain in the captured line by day may however be assumed to be about:–

(1). 3 Sections "A" Coy under an Officer
      at No. 2 Post in the Line of Observation.

(2). 3 Sections "B" Coy under an Officer
      at No. 3 Post in the Line of Observation.

(3). "C" Coy (complete) in the Line of Resistance (including about 3 Sections under an Officer at No. 4 Post)

All other units of "A" & "B" Companies and the Consolidating Party of "D" Coy would normally be withdrawn to our old line.

The defence of the whole captured line would be under OC "C" Coy whose H.Q. will be about Point B, in the centre of the Line of Resistance.

The Coy H.Q. of "A" & "B" Coys would withdraw to our old line.

During the day, "D" Coy will remain in reserve in the TUNNEL.

The units of "A" & "B" Coys withdrawn would be accommodated in HELMER CRATER dug outs.

The two Vickers guns will remain in position during the day in the Line of Resistance.

OC No. 2 Section R.E. will detail his sappers under an N.C.O. to remain in the Line of Resistance during the day.

(2).

The above orders are subject to alteration according to circumstances, and are only intended as a guide to assist Company Commanders in carrying out the necessary thinning of the line before dawn.

(See rough sketch attached.)

7th April 1917

A D Murphy Lieut Colonel
Comdg 2nd Battn The Leinster Regt

2nd Bn The Leinster Regiment

Control Posts   W.D.

The Provost Sergeant will establish Control Posts at the following points:-

(a) A Control Post of 1 N.C.O. & 3 men at the junction of HELMER Trench with KELLET trench to stop stragglers and direct traffic

(b) A Police post of 1 NCO & 8 men in rear of No 7 Post behind EMBANKMENT (about S.2.b.20.15) to collect prisoners brought in from the front line and to pass them on to Right Front Coy H.Q. in COMPANY TRENCH where they will be taken over by escorts of the 7th Northamptonshire Regt.

Jos. Thomson Lieut
Adjt Leinster Regt.

9/4/17

2nd Bn The Leinster Regiment

Orders for move from Billets to Assembly Positions

1. The Battn will move from Billets in the following order.

(a) D. Coy will leave billets at 5.30 pm, moving by platoons at 5 minutes interval and proceed via BOYEFFLES to AIX NOULETTE and thence by ARRAS Road Trench, RATION Trench to H.Q Trench, arriving there about 8 pm. Teas + Rum will be issued there + the Coy will then move to the KELLET Line in relief of Left Coy 7th Northamptonshire Regt. On arrival in KELLET line O.C D Coy will post sentries at NORTHUMBERLAND POST, ROTTENROW and in KELLET Right. The remainder of the Coy will be accommodated as follows. 1 Platoon in large dug-out South of TUNNEL, one platoon Consolidating Party, and R.E. & M.G. Detachments in TUNNEL. Sentries will be posted over all dug-outs occupied. At AIX NOULETTE O.C. D Coy will pick up the following units at 6.30 pm.

No 2 Sec 129 Coy R.E. (less 6 sappers) under 2/Lt Johnson.
1 Vickers Gun + Det 73 M.G. Coy

The above units will rendezvous at AIX NOULETTE Church at 6.15 pm.

(b) Battn H.Q. will leave billets at 6 pm + proceed via BOYEFFLES to AIX NOULETTE, thence by ARRAS Road Trench, RATION Trench to H.Q Trench, arriving there about 8.30 pm, where teas + rum will be issued. They will then move to Advanced Battn.H.Q. in KELLET Line just South of its junction with HELMER Trench.

(c) B Coy: Nos 5 + 6 Platoons will leave billets at 7 pm moving by platoons at 5 minutes interval + will proceed via main Road through AIX NOULETTE, FRENCH Dump overland to H.Q. Trench arriving there about 9 pm. After issue of teas + rum these two platoons will move to KELLET left arriving there about 10.30 pm.

(d) A Coy, Nos 1 + 2 Platoons will leave billets at 7.30 pm, moving by platoons at 5 minutes interval + will proceed via main Road to AIX NOULETTE, FRENCH Dump + overland to H.Q. Trench arriving there about 9.30 pm. After issue of teas + rum these two platoons will move to KELLET Right, arriving there about 11 pm.

No 10 Platoon "C" Coy who are detailed for Mopping up will attach one section to each of the Platoons of A + B Coys referred to in paras (c) + (d).

(e) B Coy. No 7 Platoon will leave billets at 8pm & proceed via Main Road through AIX NOULETTE, FRENCH Dump, overland to H.Q Trench arriving there about 10pm. After issue of teas & rum this platoon will move to the large dug-out at HELMER CRATER arriving there about 11 pm. Orders for its move forward to Position of Assembly from this point will be issued direct by O.C. "B" Coy as soon as the forward trenches are sufficiently clear.

(f) A Coy. No 3 Platoon will leave billets at 8.15pm & proceed via Main Road through AIX NOULETTE, FRENCH Dump, overland to H.Q. Trench arriving there about 10.15pm. After issue of teas & rum this platoon will move to the large dugout at HELMER CRATER arriving there about 11.15pm. Orders for its move forward to Position of Assembly from this point will be issued direct by O.C. "A" Coy as soon as the forward trenches are sufficiently clear.

(g) C. Coy. No 9 & 11 Platoons will leave billets at 8.30pm moving by platoons at 5 minutes interval & will proceed via Main Road through AIX NOULETTE, FRENCH Dump, overland to H.Q Trench arriving there about 10.30 pm where teas and rum will be issued. These 2 Platoons will remain in H.Q. Trench near its junction with HELMER Trench until the front trenches are sufficiently clear to move to their Assembly Positions. 6 Sappers of 129 Coy R.E. with Detachment 73rd M.G. Coy will be waiting at AIX NOULETTE Church at 8.45pm. and will be picked up by O.C. C Coy on passing.

(h) The Detachment of 12th Sherwood Foresters (Pioneers) will notify their arrival to R.S.M. Leinster Regt in H.Q Trench, ~~at 11.30pm~~ near Battn H.Q. 7th Northamptonshire Regt at 11.30pm. but will not move forward to HELMER Crater Dugouts until it is ascertained that these have been vacated by the two platoons already there.

N.B. O.C. Coys & Platoon Commanders will be careful to insure that all movements of Platoons, etc, is in the order given above & that platoons etc. do not overtake or be overtaken by other platoons of the Battalion

As the Assembly Trenches will be very congested it is most important that the above instructions are strictly adhered to.

D.D.Murphy, Lt Colonel
Comdg Leinster Regt.

Reference: Operation Order No 3.   Copy
                              by Colonel A. D. Murphy, M.C.
                              Commanding 2nd Bn. The Leinster Regt.

1. In conjunction with Operations on the VIMY RIDGE the Battalion will, on the night 9th/10th April, attack and hold the enemy's trenches in the BOIS EN HACHE Spur in co-operation with the 9th Royal Sussex Regt.

2. The objectives allotted to the Battalion are:
   (a). The enemy front line from S.2.b. 45.30 to S.2.b. 27.80.
   (b). The enemy support line from S.2.b. 45.30 to S.2.b. 60.73.

   The objectives allotted to the 9th Bn Royal Sussex Regt are the continuation to the left of these trenches to their point of junction about opposite SEBASTOPOL (M.32.d.02.28)

3. "A" and "B" Companies will capture the enemy second line (as in para 2(b)) and will each establish a strong point in this line which will be held as a Line of Observation with as weak a garrison as the situation permits.

4. "C" Company will capture and hold the enemy front line (as in para 2(a)) and will establish a strong point about S.2.b. 45.30. to protect the right flank of the attack. The enemy front line will be consolidated and will become the Line of Resistance. A central strong point (No. 3) will be established at S.2.b. 20.45.

5. "D" Company (less one platoon) will be in General Reserve and will be accommodated in the Tunnel in rear of NORTHUMBERLAND POST. One platoon "D" Company will be attached to 129th Co. R.E. as consolidating party for the enemy front line.

6. Immediately each objective is gained, patrols will be pushed forward under cover of

(2)

and Bombing Posts will be established to cover the work of consolidation. Connecting Posts to keep touch between Companies and the Battalion on our left will be established between Strong Points and between the two objectives.

7. Before dawn both the Line of Observation and the Line of Resistance will be thinned out, as far as the situation permits, in accordance with instructions already issued to Os.C. Companies. From the time that the withdrawal commences, the defence of the whole of the captured trenches will devolve on O.C. "C" Company, whose Headquarters will be established in the vicinity of Point B. (S.2.b. ...45.).

8. Companies will commence to assemble outside our own wire at ZERO – 60. Owing to the marked alertness of the enemy the assembly must be very slowly and carefully carried out. From ZERO – 60 to ZERO our artillery will carry out a slow bombardment of the enemy front line on an extended front.

9. At ZERO hour, our artillery barrage will become intense and the Assaulting Companies will advance into NO MAN'S LAND getting as far forward as our barrage permits. At ZERO + 10 the barrage will lift to the enemy second line and Companies will advance again as far as possible, the two leading lines pushing on in the direction of the second objective and the supporting lines capturing first objective. At ZERO + 25, the barrage will lift behind the enemy second line

(3)

line and the second objective will be
consolidated and captured.

10. As the hours of darkness after ZERO
hour will be short, no time must be lost
in commencing the important work of
consolidation. Every man not especially
detailed for observation or defence must
assist in the work of making the captured
trenches defensible.

11. The following units are attached to
the Battalion:—

(a) No. 2 Section 129th Co. R.E. under Lieut.
Johnson. This Section (less 6 men, now attached
to "C" Company) will remain in dug-outs in
the KELLET line during the attack. It will
be ordered to advance to the enemy front
line, to assist in the work of consolidation as
soon as the hostile barrage permits. The
Platoon of "D" Company detailed as consolidating party will be attached to this Section
and will be under the orders of Lieut. Johnson.

(b) Two guns (with detachments) of 73rd
M.G. Company under —————. One gun
will be attached to 4 Platoon of "C" Company
and will move with this Platoon to No. 1
Post under the orders of Lieut. Quinlan.
One gun will be attached to "D" Company
and will move to the line of resistance
as soon as the situation permits.

(c) Two guns (with detachments) of 73rd
L.T.M. Battery under —————.
These guns will come into position before
ZERO hour behind the EMBANKMENT about
S.2.a.80.15. and will co-operate with the attack

(4)

... or from this point.

(d) Half Company of 12th Sherwood Foresters (Pioneers) under ... ... will assemble in HELMER CRATER ... by 12 midnight. As soon as the situation permits they will move forward and will construct a communication trench from NORTHUMBERLAND ... to the vicinity of Point B (2.b.20.45).

12. During the attack, the 7th Northamptonshire Regiment will continue to hold our present front line by a series of Lewis Gun Posts.

13. Platoon Flags will be utilised by day to show the position of our Posts to our artillery. The Platoon Flag has no meaning unless waved backwards and towards our line. Platoon Runners will carry these flags.

14. The S.O.S. Signal, by night or day, will be a succession of White Very Lights fired back horizontally towards the rear.

15. The arrangements for communication and a List of CODE Words to be used are given in Appendix A.

16. The Medical Arrangements and those for the Disposal of Prisoners, as well as the arrangements for the collection and supply of ... and the orders regarding equipment, etc., have already been notified in Divisional Memorandum No. 1.

17. Orders for the move of the Battalion from present billets will be issued tomorrow.

APPENDIX A.

Communications

1. Two Signallers equipped with visual apparatus will go forward with the leading Platoons of each Assaulting Company.

2. A Power Buzzer will go forward with "C" Company and will be installed about Point B (S.2.b.20.45.). As all messages sent on the Power Buzzer can be picked up by the enemy all messages will be in code except in case of extreme emergency.

3. One runner will go forward with each Platoon Headquarters and four runners with each Company H.Q. Runners will wear a special badge on the left upper arm.

4. Verbal messages are not to be sent and will be disregarded.

5. All Officers and N.C.O's are to carry notebooks and pencils.

6. The following code words will be used:-

(a) When Coys have reached the enemy's front line i.e. The Line of Resistance . . . . DICK.

(b) When Coys have reached the enemy's second line i.e. The Line of Observation . . . . ETHEL

(c) Ammunition required . . . . S.A.A.
    Bombs required . . . . MILLS
    Enemy concentrating on right . . . . MARK.RIGHT.
      "   "   "   left . . . . MARK.LEFT.
    Barrage too close . . . . CLOSE.
    Reinforcements wanted . . . . MORE

In addition situation reports at least every hour are expected from Companies.

O.C. "C" Coy will take forward the B.A.B. Code Book, and will use this code when sending any message other than the above by Power Buzzer.

The B.A.B. Code correction and the above Code Words are to be committed to memory by all Officers.

Reference
1/10,000
Sheet 36.c.SW3

Operation Order No. 3.
by
Lt. Colonel A. D. MURPHY. M.C.
Commanding 2nd Bn. The Leinster Regt.

Copy

1. In conjunction with Operations on the VIMY RIDGE the Battalion will, on the night 9th/10th April, attack and hold the enemy's trenches on the BOIS EN HACHE Spur in co-operation with the 9th Royal Sussex Regt.

2. The objectives allotted to the Battalion are:—
   (a). The enemy front line from S.2.b. 45.20 to S.2.b. 37.80.
   (b). The enemy support line from S.2.b. 45.30 to S.2.b. 60.73.

   The objectives allotted to the 9th Bn Royal Sussex Regt are the continuation to the left of these trenches to their point of junction about opposite SEBASTOPOL (M.32.d.02.28)

3. "A" and "B" Companies will capture the enemy second line (as in para 2.b.) and will each establish a strong point in this line which will be held as a Line of Observation with a weak garrison as the situation permits.

4. "C" Company will capture and hold the enemy front line (as in para 2.a.) and will establish a strong point about S.2.b. 40.30 to protect the right flank of the attack. The enemy front line will be consolidated and will become the Line of Resistance. A central strong point (R.?) will be established about S.2.b. 20.45.

5. "D" Company (less one platoon) will be in General Reserve and will be accommodated in the tunnel in rear of NORTHUMBERLAND POST. One platoon "D" Company will be attached to 254th Co. R.E. as consolidating party for the enemy front line.

6. Immediately each objective is gained, patrols will be pushed forward under our barrage

(2)

and Bombing Posts will be established to cover the work of consolidation. Connecting Posts to keep touch between Companies and the Battalion on our left will be established between Strong Points and between the two objectives

7. Before dawn both the Line of Observation and the Line of Resistance will be thinned out, as far as the situation permits, in accordance with instructions already issued to Os. C. Companies. From the time that the withdrawal commences the defence of the whole of the captured trenches will devolve on O.C. "C" Company, whose Headquarters will be established in the vicinity of Point B. (S.2.b.20.45.).

8. Companies will commence to assemble outside our own wire at ZERO – 60. Owing to the marked alertness of the enemy the assembly must be very slowly and carefully carried out. From ZERO – 60 to ZERO our artillery will carry out a slow bombardment of the enemy front line on an extended front.

9. At ZERO hour, our artillery barrage will become intense and the Assaulting Companies will advance into NO MAN'S LAND getting as far forward as our barrage permits. At ZERO + 10, the barrage will lift to the enemy second line and Companies will advance again as far as possible, the two leading lines pushing on in the direction of the second objective and the succeeding lines capturing the first objective. At ZERO + 25, the barrage will lift behind the enemy second line

(3)

forward the second objective will be
reached and captured.

10. As the hours of darkness after ZERO
hour will be short, no time must be lost
in commencing the important work of
consolidation. Every man not actually
detailed for observation or defence must
assist in the work of making the captured
trench defensible.

11. The following units are attached to
our Battalion:-

(a) No 2. Section 129th Co. R.E. under Lieut
Johnson. This Section (less 6 sappers attached to "C" Company) will remain in dug-outs in
the KELLEY line during the attack but will
be ordered to advance to the enemy front
line to assist in the work of consolidation as
soon as the hostile barrage permits. The
Platoon of "D" Company detailed as consolidating party will be attached to this Section
and will be under the orders of Lieut Johnson.

(b). Two guns (with detachments) of 73rd
M.G. Company under.   One gun
will be attached to No.1 Platoon of C Company
and will move with this Platoon. No 2.
gun under the orders of Lieut Chambers
One gun will be attached to "D" Company
and will move to the line of Resistance
as soon as the situation permits.

(c). Two guns (with detachments) of 73rd
L.T.M. Battery under.
These guns will come into position before
ZERO hour behind the EMBANKMENT about
S.2.b.30.15. and will co-operate with the
attack.

attack from this point.

(b) Half Company of 12th Bhawalpore Lancers (Pioneers), under their O.C. will assemble in HELMER CRATER by 12 midnight. As soon as the situation permits they will move forward and will construct a communication trench from NORTHUMBERLAND POST to the vicinity of Point B (6. 20.d.5)

12. During the attack, the 7th Northampton Regiment will continue to hold our present front line by a series of Lewis Gun Posts.

13. Platoon Flags will be utilised by day to show the position of our Posts to our Artillery. The Platoon Flag has no meaning unless waved backwards & forwards our line. Platoon Runners will carry these flags.

14. The S.O.S. Signal by night or day, will be a succession of White Very Lights fired back horizontally towards the rear.

15. The arrangements for communication and a list of CODE Words to be used are given in Appendix A.

16. The Medical Arrangements and those for the Disposal of Prisoners, as well as, the arrangements for the collection and supply of water and the orders regarding equipment, etc, have already been notified in Preliminary Memorandum No.1.

17. Orders for the move of the Battalion from present billets will be issued tomorrow.

18.

will be
TUNNEL all
to this

(3)

18. All watches will be synchronised at the following places and hours:—

(a) POST 10 Battn. Orderly Room at 10 a.m., 2 pm and 6 pm. An Officer from each Company will report to the Adjutant at these hours.

(b) HEADQUARTERS TRENCH — Battalion Headquarters 7th Bn. Northamptonshire Regt. at 12 midnight.
Lieut. R.J. Porter will report to the Brigade Signal Officer at above place at this hour, and will be responsible that synchronised time is delivered to all Officers before 1.00 a.m.

19. Battalion Headquarters will be established at the present Left Company Headquarters 7th Bn. Northamptonshire Regt. in KELLY TRENCH just South of its junction with HELMER TRENCH by 11 p.m.

                                    Thomson   Lieutenant
                                    7th Bn. The Border Regiment.

1. "A" Coy
2. "B" Coy
3. "C" Coy
4. D Coy
5. Intelligence Officer
6. Quartermaster
7. OC 1st Coy R.E.
8. OC 73rd L.T.M. Battery
9. OC 73rd M.G. Company
10. OC 9th Suffolk Divn Cyc.
11. Brigade Headquarters
12. File
13. War Diary
14. R.S.O.
15. OC 10th Sherwood Foresters.

Operation Order No.
Lt.Colonel A.D. Murphy M.C.
Comdg 2nd Bn Leinster Regiment
11th April 1917.

1. The attack on the BOIS-EN-HACHE Ridge arranged for the night 9th/10th April 1917, will take place tonight. ZERO hour will be at 2 am.

The 4th Canadian Division will attack the PIMPLE in co-operation with the attack of the 73rd Brigade. The 50th Canadian Battalion will be operating on our immediate right.

2. The 17th Infantry Brigade will, if the wind is favourable, discharge smoke along the Brigade front, from ZERO hour onwards, and will co-operate with machine-gun fire.

3. All arrangements previously made for the night 9th/10th April will hold good for tonight, except that the R.E. & M.G. Detachments will rendezvous at FRENCH DUMP at 6.30 pm and 9 pm instead of at AIX NOULETTE Church at 6.15 pm and 8.45 pm.

4. Watches will be synchronised at Orderly Room at 2 pm and 5.30 pm.

At midnight 2/L W.J Porter will report for correct time at Batln H.Q. 7th Bn Northamptonshire Regt in HEADQUARTER TRENCH, and will be responsible for delivering synchronised time to all Officers at their Point of Assembly.

A.D Murphy Lt Colonel
Commanding 2nd Bn Leinster Regt

Copy No 1 - A Coy   Copy No 6. Quartermaster
  "   - 2. B Coy   "   " 7 Brigade H.Q.
  "   - 3 C Coy   "   " 8. File
  "   - 4 D Coy   "   " 9 War Diary
  "   - 5 2/Lt J Porter   "   " 10 R.S.M.

O.C. Coy.
R.T.O.
Quartermaster

Leinster No.
P. 522.

1. In order to conform with the Operations of the 4th Canadian Division on the PIMPLE. ZERO hour for our attack has now been altered to 5 a.m. instead of 2 a.m.

2. All previous orders still hold good, but all timings will be three hours later than those given in Operation Orders and subsequent Instructions issued.

3. All movement from present billets will now be by Main Road to AIX NOULETTE. "D" Coy & "H.Q." Coy will therefore parade at 9 pm and 9.30 pm. respectively

4. No 3 Platoon "A" Coy will parade at 11.10 pm.

5. With the above exceptions all platoons will parade three hours later than stated in "Orders for move from Billets to Assembly Positions".

6. The R.T.O will arrange for a limber for Lewis Guns to parade with each Coy & follow the Coy as far as the Trench Dump on ARRAS ROAD. The Mess Cart will be at Battn. H.Q at 9.30 pm. Coy Commanders' horses will parade with their Coys. H.Q. horses will be at the mess at 10 pm.

7. In the case of all Coys etc, the hours given for parade are the hours at which the leading platoon of each Company should pass the level crossing just East of Battn Headquarters

Issued. 4.15 pm.
11.4.1917.

Jas Plowman Lieut
Adj Leinster Regt

"C" Form (Original). Army Form C. 2123.
MESSAGES AND SIGNALS. No. of Message

Prefix	Code	Words	Received	Sent, or sent out	Office Stamp
Charges to collect	£ s. d.		From... By...	At...........m. To........... By J. Watson	
Service Instructions. Oct 3					

Handed in at.................... Office.........m. Received 11.35 .. m.

TO Turkey

*Sender's Number	Day of Month	In reply to Number	A A A
435	12		

Following message received a a a
C in C congratulates the troops
on their success today a a a
Please convey this message to
all ranks

FROM
PLACE & TIME   Tment

Operation Order No. [?] (a)   Copy No. 10
                                      War Diary

[?] Bn. The [?] India Regt.

                                      5 April 1917

1. The 46th Division is to be relieved by the 4th
Division commencing today. On relief the 46th
Division will join the I Corps and will be
[?] into rest in ST. HILAIRE Area.

2. This Battalion will move this afternoon to billets
at HOUCHIN.

3. Coys will leave at 2.30 pm in the following
order and move independently to BRACQUEMONT
Church L.q.d.2.1

        H.Q. Coy
        D. Coy
        C. Coy
        B. Coy
        A. Coy
        [?] [?]
        Transport

Lewis & L[?] teams will parade with H.Q. Coy.
4. The Divl Band will join the Battn at 3.15 pm
and the march will be continued via NOEUX-LES-MINES and
Road Junction K.R.C.1.3 to HOUCHIN.

5. The usual Billeting Party will parade at 11.30 am,
(under instructions already issued) under the Quartermaster.

6. Officers Kits and ground sheets or waterproof
capes will be stacked at Q.M. Stores not later than
1 pm & will be collected there by Regtl Transport.
Blankets will be stacked at the same place as soon
as possible & will be conveyed to billets by lorry.
The Mess Cart will collect the Officers' Mess Stores
commencing at H.Q. Mess at 2 pm.

(kit blankets to be not ground sheets or waterproof capes may be worn)

Issued at 11.0 am
                        [signature]
                        Cmdg [?] Bn The [?] Regt

Operation Order No 5
by
Lt Colonel A. D. Murphy M.C.
Comdg 2nd Bn The Leinster Regiment

18th April 1917

1. The Battalion will march to AUCHEL tomorrow 19th inst as under:-

Starting Point Cross Roads. K.15.C.2.8.
Route. Road junction J.17.b.8.8. - MARLES-LES-MINES - LOZINGHEM. Time 10.10 am. Order of march.

   H.Q. Coy.
   "A" Coy.
   "C" Coy.
   "B" Coy.
   "D" Coy.
   Training Platoon
   Transport.

2. The march to Rest Area will be continued on 20th inst.

3. All baggage for loading on wagons or lorries will be stacked at Camp by 9.15 am. Mess stores will be ready for collection by 9.45 am.

4. The usual billeting party will parade under the Quartermaster at the Camp at 9.30am.

5. Sick parade will be at 7.30 am.

Issued at 11.45pm
18/4/17.

E. Plowman Lt & Adjt for Lt Colonel
Comdg 2nd Bn The Leinster Regt.

Copy No 1. A Coy
  2. B Coy
  3. C Coy
  4. D Coy
  5. Q'Mr
  6. R.T.O
  7. L.G.O
  8. R.S.M.
  9. Training Platoon

Copy No 10. File
Copy No 11. War Diary
 No 12. H.Q. Coy.
 No 13. Adjutant
 No 14. C.O.

Operation Order No.
                                    (C 26.6.5.0)

1. The Battalion will march to LAIRES tomorrow 26th inst as under:
    Starting Point, Church at CAUCHY-A-LA-TOUR
Time 9.45am   Order of march
        H.Q. Coy
        "C" Coy
        "D" Coy
        "B" Coy
        "A" Coy
        Training Platoon
        Transport.

Route CAUCHY-A-LA-TOUR — FERFAY — AMETTES — FONTAINE
LES HERMANS — LIGNIN PALFART.

2. Dinners will be served on the line of march near FONTAINE-LES-HERMANS about 12.30pm

3. All Officers' baggage will be stacked outside Officers' billets at 8.30am and collected under arrangements to be made by the R.T.O. Blankets will be stacked outside Q.M Stores by 8.30am

    Officers' Mess boxes will be ready for collection by 9am.

                            Jas. Plowman Lieut & Adjutant
Issued at 7pm   Cmdg 2nd Bn 3rd /Munster Regt

Copy No 1. "A" Coy ✓   Copy No 11. Training Platoon ✓
     2. "B"   ✓   12. War Diary ✓
     3. "C"   ✓   13. File ✓
     4. "D"   ✓   14. L.G. Officer
     5. C.O   ✓
     6. Adj   ✓
     7. R.T.O ✓
     8. Q'M' ✓
     9. R.M   ✓
    10. H.Q Coy ✓

Operation Order No 7
by
Lt Col A.D. Murphy M.C.
Comdg Leinster Regt
26th April 1917

1. The 73rd I. Bde will move by stages to NOEUX-LES-MINES Area today
2. The Battn will halt tonight at AUCHEL
3. As no extra transport is available, all heavy baggage will be left at the Q.M Stores.
   Each Coy will detail one man to remain behind in charge of Stores and O.C. "D" Coy will detail a L.Cpl. to be in charge of this party, which will have rations for 27th & 28th.
4. Officers' Kits & ground sheets will be ready for collection at Coy Billets by 12 noon
   Officers' mess Stores will be ready at 12.45 pm
5. The usual Billeting Party under the Qr Mr will parade at 1 pm. at the Church
6. Dinners will be served at 12.15 pm.

10.45 am.

Jas Plowman Lieut
Adjt Leinster Regt

Copy No 1.	A Coy	Copy No 14. War Diary
2	B Coy
3	C Coy
4	D Coy
5	L.G.O
6	Qr Mr
7	R.T.O
8	R.S.M
9	Trg Platoon
10	H.Q. Coy
11	C.O.
12	Adjt
13	File

Headquarters,
24th. Division.

I Corps No.1117/14/6 (G.a.). 12.4.17.
24th. Divn.No. G.X.482/41.
dated 12. 4. 17.

The Corps Commander wishes his thanks conveyed to the Officers and men of the 9th. Battalion The Royal Sussex Regiment and the 2nd. Battalion The Leinster Regiment of the success of their attack on the BOIS EN HACHE. The Corps Commander fully appreciates the difficulties of weather and ground under which the attack was carried out, but the determination of all ranks to get in with the bayonet overcame these difficulties and has again proved that British Infantry are irresistable at close quarters.

The Corps Commander also wishes to express his appreciation of the work done by the Artillery in supporting the attack. The siting of the trenches rendered the barrage particularly difficult to put on but this difficulty proved only an obstacle to be overcome. The counter battery work was very effective and contributed very greatly to the success of the operation.

The Corps Commander further wishes to express his thanks to the Brigade and Divisional Staffs for the care and foresight with which the scheme was drawn up and for the energy with which all difficulties were met and surmounted.

12. 4. 17.
Sd. G.V.HORDERN. Brig. General,
General Staff, I Corps.

Officer Commanding,
9th. Royal Sussex Regt.
2nd. Leinster Regt.

73rd. I.B. NO.

B.M.268.

Forwarded for the information of the Officers, N.C.O's and men who successfully and gallantly carried out the attack this morning. I have little to add to the remarks of the Corps Commander except to say that there is no one who appreciates their bravery and all the hard work they have done more than I do.

H.Q. 73 I.B.
12. 4. 17.
Brigadier General,
Commanding 73rd. Infantry Brigade.

The Commanding Officer offers his congratulations to the Officers, Warrant Officers, N.C.Os and men of the Battalion on their splendid behaviour during the attack on the Bois-en-Hache spur on the 12th inst. The attack was carried out under the most trying conditions but the gallantry, endurance and spirit of all ranks were beyond praise. The success of this operation has had a very great and far reaching effect on the enemy and almost certainly brought about his withdrawal before it was intended.

Special Order of the Day
by
Major General J.E. Capper C.B
Commanding 24th Division
April 19th 1917.

The Divisional Commander is proud to have to communicate the following messages to the Troops under his command:-

From The First Army Commander.
to G.O.C. 1st Corps.

I am anxious to express to you, the Divisional and other Commanders, and to all ranks, my appreciation of the important part taken by the I Corps in the recent operations.

The success of the counter battery work carried out by the Artillery is proved by inspection of the hostile gun emplacements in LIEVIEN. So satisfactory result could only have been attained by great devotion to duty on the part of all ranks of the Royal Artillery and Royal Flying Corps, combined with scientific and accurate work by the Sound Ranging Sections, ground observers and others concerned with the location of the hostile batteries.

The 24th Division deserves great credit, not only for the skilful capture of BOIS-EN-HACHE, but also for the promptitude and determination with which they have followed up the retirement of the enemy through an area presenting so many difficulties. This is more noteworthy when it is remembered that this Division has spent practically the whole winter & Spring in a trying section of the trenches.

From G.O.C. 1st Corps.
To The 24th Division

On the departure of the 24th Division, I wish to express to Major General Capper C.B, the 24th Divisional and other Staffs, and to all ranks, my high appreciation of the work done by the Division during the time I have had the honour to command the I Corps.

During this time the 24th Division have shewn themselves possessed of the highest military qualities. In trench warfare they have been most tenacious in defence, and enterprising in raids; and, when the opportunity was afforded by the retirement of the enemy, most dashing in offence.

In bidding good-bye to the Division, I wish it all luck in the future.

(sd) J. Doyle. Lt.Colonel
A.A. + Q.M.G. 24th Division

Issued to Corps etc.
20/4/17.

War Diary

The following message has been received from General Sir H.C.O. Plumer, G.C.M.G., K.C.B., A.D.C. Commanding Second Army :-

"To General Capper,
24th Division.

Commander and Staff Second Army delighted to hear of your success AAA many congratulations to you and your Division."

J.D.Doyle
Lieut-Colonel,
A.A.&Q.M.G., 24th Division.

24th Divn. H.Q.
17th April 1917.

24th. Division.

No. 1117/10/4 (G.b.) 16th. April, 1917.

    The Commander-in-Chief has desired me to express to the 6th. and 24th. Divisions and Heavy Artillery, I Corps, his appreciation of the able and energetic manner in which the enemy has been pressed during his retirement. Our advance has been bold and methodical and has in consequence succeeded with a minimum of casualties.
    The operation now being carried out by the I Corps is of considerable value to the General Plan.
    The Corps Commander in making known the appreciation of the C.-in-C., wishes at the same time to express his own thanks to all ranks for the very good work which has been done.

        sd.   H.R. SANDILANDS, Major G.S.
                          for Brig. General.
                          General Staff, I Corps.

- 2 -

24th. Division. No. G. 608.

Infantry Brigade.

    Herewith 100 copies for distribution to units under your command.

                          Captain. General Staff.
                            24th. Division.

16-4-1917.

Per Stephen) RAME
" Dennis

With reference to the successful operations which took place on this front on the morning of April 12th, resulting in the capture of "The PIMPLE" by the 4th Canadian Division and "The BOIS EN HACHE" by the 9th Bn. Royal Sussex Regt., and the 2nd Bn. Leinster Regt., 73rd Infantry Bde., 24th Division, the following message has been received from the Commander in Chief via the I Corps.

"Please convey to the 24th Division and 4th Canadian Division congratulations on the success of their operations this morning and my appreciation of the gallantry and skill shewn by the troops engaged AAA ends".

H. Boyd-Rochfort
Captain,
General Staff.
24th Division.

13th April. 1917.

Army Form C. 2118

WAR DIARY
or
INTELLIGENCE SUMMARY.
(Erase heading not required.)

War Diary of
1st Battalion The Leinster Regt
for the month of
May 1917

Vol 34

WAR DIARY
or
INTELLIGENCE SUMMARY.

Army Form C. 2118.

Place	Date	Hour	Summary of Events and Information	Remarks and references to Appendices
HOOGHE	MAY 1	10-15am	Shelling. The J.F.B. 44th Div. & O.C. 6 2nd Bde. visited the Batln.	J.P.
"	2		"	J.P.
"	3		"	J.P.
"	4		" 2 men found 10 R wounded (accidental)	J.P.
"	5		Training	J.P.
"	6		8 Officers joined	J.P.
"	7		" 2 O.R.	J.P.
"	8			J.P.
"	9	10-30am	Left HOOGHE & marched BELLERIVE to join 2nd Group. arrived 11am	J.P.
BELLERIVE	10	11am	BELLERIVE " Moved to Le Bas. arrived about 6am. Batt. H.Q. (ECHEBECQUE STN.)	J.P.
Le BAS	11		Billets. 1 officer joined	J.P.
"	12	11am	Left Le BAS. & marched to Billets near E. OSTEENVOORDE. arrived about 6pm.	J.P.
OSTEENVOORDE	13		Billets. Visited by the officers & men of the H.Q. 6 Bgd. Battn. & 2nd Battn. V	J.P.
"	14	7pm	7 A Bn. The battalion now forms part of I Corps, Second Army (Hut 29) Left OSTEENVOORDE & proceeded to Reserve Corps (from L.P.O.A.) near BENSEBEEN 3 officers & 68 O.R. remained behind by Tim.DIV (?)	J.P.

2353 Wt. W2544/1454 700,000 5/15 D. D. & L. A.D.S.S./Forms/C.2118.

WAR DIARY

Place	Date	Hour	Summary of Events and Information	Remarks and references to Appendices
EVILLERS CAMP W.13007	15		Demolished camps.	A.R.
"	16		Continued work under orders of C.R.E. II Corps. (7am & 7-8 pm)	A.R.
"	17		2nd Lt. Col. Hughes R.E. ordered to take over temporary command of Group.	A.R.
			Battn from Major R.H. Roper. Major R.A. Ruffe assumed command of the Battn.	
			1 hour drill taken up to 10.15 am.	
"	18		Working parties as usual. W.O.R. joined Training Batts.	A.R.
"	19		2nd Lt. H. Brown rejoined D. & Training Batts. (Wenvoeures)	A.R.
"	20		G. Cole and C. Dutaing Coy L.Cpl V.S.H.	
			The C.O. Coy Officers & Commdrs Nominal Roll & Ord. area & O.R. reported formed T. Battn. A.O.R. went to Nominal of B. and Training Battn. 2 Officers.	
			Battn from T. Battn.	
"	21		Usual work parties for the C.O.B. Majors & D. Battn.	A.R.
"	22		" Ex Off. of Coy Commanders nominated for D.A. area	A.R.
"	23		"	A.R.
"	24		Col. of Coy Commdrs & two N.C.O.s reconnoitred	A.R.
			17th Div area	

Army Form C. 2118.

WAR DIARY
or
INTELLIGENCE SUMMARY.
(Erase heading not required.)

Instructions regarding War Diaries and Intelligence Summaries are contained in F. S. Regs., Part II. and the Staff Manual respectively. Title pages will be prepared in manuscript.

Place	Date	Hour	Summary of Events and Information	Remarks and references to Appendices
Devonport Camp Witley	25		Barker, Captain, 1st Col. U.D. Brought 1st Group the Batts.	AP
"	26		" 11 Officers & 1800 joined Battn from Railway Batt.	AP
"	27		" 161 OR. reinforcements joined.	AP
"	28	4.00am	" 60 Officers Bn Command 2 COs ordered friends & moved to He.Q. Div. arca (Right Batt. front)	AP
"	29		Instructions to the Coy/o Commander make 30.Th. Batt. Left Batt. to filled and camp at No. 3. C.L.L. Bear Halloween Camp.	AP
"	30		Workington transport moved to camp near Halloween	AP
"	31		" 240 O.W.L. Draftees joined Bn.	AP
			Effective Strength of the Battn. 35 Officers & 920 OR. French Strength " " 26 Officers & 730 OR.	AP

A.J. Murphy L/Col.
Comg 2nd Can. C. Bn.

2353 Wt. W2544/1454 700,000 5/15 D. D. & L. A.D.S.S./Forms/C. 2118.

Army Form C. 2118.

WAR DIARY

~~INTELLIGENCE SUMMARY.~~
(*Erase heading not required.*)

Vol 36

Place	Date	Hour	Summary of Events and Information	Remarks and references to Appendices
Contentent			2nd Bn Leinster Regiment for the month of June 1914	

Army Form C. 2118.

WAR DIARY
or
INTELLIGENCE SUMMARY.

(Erase heading not required.)

Instructions regarding War Diaries and Intelligence Summaries are contained in F.S. Regs., Part II. and the Staff Manual respectively. Title pages will be prepared in manuscript.

Place	Date	Hour	Summary of Events and Information	Remarks and references to Appendices
Devonshire Camp	June 1-6-17		Battn in Devonshire Camp.	Obey.
STEENVOORDE	2	7am	Battn left camp and moved to Mr. STEENVOORDE area. Major Freeman joined from 15th DLI.	Obey.
		2 pm	Arrived in billets 2 miles NORTH of STEENVOORDE. 5 mm reinforcements joined.	Obey.
"	3		Billets. Practised attack.	Obey.
"	4	7pm	Left billets and marched to a camp near LYSSENTHOEK arrived about 11pm.	Obey.
"	5	11pm	Left camp and proceeded to OTTAWA camp near OUDERDOM arriving about 1.30am	Obey.
OTTAWA Camp	6	12 mn	The Battn left the camp and proceeded to assembly trenches in the vicinity of SWAN CHATEAU and CAFE BELGE. Battn HQ situated at Sheet 28NW H30a1.4. Arrived about 2.15 AM. During the move enemy artillery very active wing gas + tear shells. 5 men of Battn gased.	Obey.
Ouderdom	7	3.10am	Our artillery opened a terrific bombardment which lasted for about an hour.	
		12 noon	Battn left Assembly positions moving in artillery formation in the following order BTD, ETA forward old FRENCH TRENCH & ECLUSE TRENCH. Arrived there about 2.15 pm. Battn HQ was established at Z 32 d 4.2 Sheet 28 NW. Our artillery very active.	
		2.30pm	Battn left OLD FRENCH TRENCH & ECLUSE TRENCH & proceeded in artillery	

2353 Wt. W2544/1454 500,000 5/15 D. D. & L.   A.D.S.S./Forms/C. 2118.

WAR DIARY or INTELLIGENCE SUMMARY

Army Form C.2118.

Place	Date	Hour	Summary of Events and Information	Remarks and references to Appendices
	8.		formation to O.3 central. Arrived about 3.30pm. Dispositions of the Battn. "B" "D" Coys OLD GERMAN front line in O.3.d. "A" "B" Coys SOUTH and EAST of copse at O.3 central. Battn HQ at O.3.d.0.9. At 5.20pm "C" "D" Coys were ordered to move forward about 300 yds. "A" "B" Coys moved up into old positions of "C" "D" Coys. Battn HQ in vicinity of RUINED FARM. Patrols pushed forward to keep touch with leading Battn. 2nd Lt R.E. Warner rejoined from Hosp.	RWJ
		3 AM	O.O. received from Bde. 7 Battn moved to support 9th Royal Sussex + 13th Middlesex at 3.30am. Relieved 13th London Regt in BLACK LINE arriving about 5.30am and occupying OBLONG ALLEY & OBLONG AVENUE. Battn HQ at O + 0.5.5. "A" + "B" Coys in OBLONG RESERVE. "B" Coy N.W. of DAMMSTRASSE. "D" Coy near ruined stables. Hostile artillery very active on "C" "D" Coys + Bn. HQ. 8.45pm our artillery very active. The enemy replied by shelling back area. Bombardment lasted till 11pm when hostile fire practically ceased. Our artillery very active during night. At 9.30pm found working party for 13th Middlesex. 2/Lt B. Sturt & 2/Lt Heather wounded in action.	RWJ
	9.		Artillery active. 9.30pm "D" Coy on work continuing communication trench from the east of OBLONG RESERVE. To O.10.C.55.55. along edge of wood. 10pm working party reported to 13th Middlesex at DEABSKE FARM. 2/Lt M. O'Brien wounded in action.	RWJ

WAR DIARY
or
INTELLIGENCE SUMMARY.
(Erase heading not required.)

Army Form C. 2118.

Place	Date	Hour	Summary of Events and Information	Remarks and references to Appendices
	10		Artillery active. Improving positions.	ay.
	11		Very quiet. Battn relieved by 2 Coys of 365 Royal Fusiliers at 4.30 pm. Relief completed at 5.20 pm. Battn arrived & bivouacked at OTTAWA CAMP (7254). 0 R's killed & 9 0 R's in action.)	ay.
OTTAWA Camp	12		Remained in bivouacks near OTTAWA CAMP. 8916 Cpl J. Cunningham awarded the Victoria Cross (posthumous award) for gallantry in action on 12th April 1917, Divisional Routine Orders dated 11/5/17. The u/m Officers & NCO's were mentioned in despatches supplement to London Gazette dated 25/5/17, Major J.R. French, Lt-QM H.O. Squire, 7898 Dolan Sgt Phelan, 7244 Sgt McCarthy.	
n. OOSEROOM.			17 OR's joined Battn.	ay
Micmac	13.	6 pm	Left OTTAWA Camp for MICMAC CAMP. Arrived in MICMAC CAMP at 6.45 pm.	ay
	14		Bivouacked in MICMAC CAMP. 6 OR's joined Battn. Major Freeman in Command of Battn.	ay
	15.	7.15 pm	Battn left MICMAC Camp for trenches near Hill 60. Battn HQ arrived 12.30 am. Relief completed 4.30 am. Battn relieved the 8th Buffs. Disposition:- Front line At "E" Coy, Lt "D" Coy. In reserve A" "B" Coys.	ay.
	16.		Throughout the morning, enemy shelled left portion of BATTLE WOOD. Afternoon quiet. 6 pm – 7 pm heavy shelling of support lines. 9.30 pm – 11.30 pm heavy	

WAR DIARY
or
INTELLIGENCE SUMMARY.
(Erase heading not required.)

Army Form C. 2118.

Place	Date	Hour	Summary of Events and Information	Remarks and references to Appendices
	17.	7.31am	Bombardment of all trenches by enemy. Casualties slight. Four enemy aeroplanes flying low over our lines machine gunned our trenches – no casualties. 9.20 am nine enemy aeroplanes came over flying at a great height, but were driven off by our anti-aircraft fire & our planes. During morning enemy shelled Batln. H.Q. and our forward battery positions. 8.10 pm six enemy planes over our line were driven off by anti-aircraft fire. Patrol under Lieut W.J. Parla reconnoitred front, & encountered no enemy.	Ques.
	18.	1.30 am	2 Huns belonging to 179th I.R. were captured by 100s Pte Bassitz? (60 orderly) F.O.O. & orderly were captured by Brigade Commander Lt Col A.D. Murphy M.C. & the Brigade Major about 3:30 am. At 7:30 am enemy heavy artillery fired on our batteries. Fairly quiet throughout day. 3pm–5pm our artillery fired on enemy batteries. 7 pm enemy shelled our trenches & vicinity of Battn H.Q. Capt F.B. Bradock, 2/Lt G.H. Kennon 2/Lt R.O.W. Butler joined Battn.	Ques.
	19.	1.30 am	Enemy sent up "Golden Rain" very light signals & heavy bombardment. "Stand to" was ordered, bombardment ceased at 2:50 am when "stand down" was ordered.	Rees.

WAR DIARY
INTELLIGENCE SUMMARY

Army Form C. 2118.

Place	Date	Hour	Summary of Events and Information	Remarks and references to Appendices
	19	6-7 am	Hostile aircraft active. One enemy plane flying low over our trenches was engaged and driven off by our machine gun + rifle fire. 2 pm enemy shelled Battn HQ heavily. 5-6 pm enemy shelling on front line Battn HQ. Casualties for period 15th – 19th killed OR's 15 wounded 42. 19 OR's joined Battn. Relief by 13th Middlesex commenced at 10 pm. Relief completed at 12.30 am.	Ack.
DICKEBUSCH	20	2 am	Arrived in camp (DICKEBUSCH) "A" Coy remained as garrison on SPOIL BANK.	Ack.
	21	7.30 pm	Enemy shelled camp. Battn had any wounded. 10 R. killed + OR's wounded.	Ack.
	22		Remained in same camp. Received shelling round camp until 5.30 pm.	Ack.
OUDERDOM			Battn moved to HUBERTUSHOEK camp arrived about 6.30 pm.	Ack.
"	23		Battn in HUBERTUSHOEK camp. Working party of 125 men under 2 Coys Lignell 7.30 pm. 2/Lts Barker, Keogh, Haresham Moore joined Battn.	Ack.
	24		ditto	Ack.
	25		ditto	Ack.
VIERSTRAAT	26	11 am	Battn left camp + proceeded to N 10 b 8.9 to relieve 12th D.L.I. Relief complete 12 noon. 73rd Bde less 2/Krinklets moved down to rest area. Battn attached to 17th Bde. work under X Corps Signals. 1 Officer + 40 men from each other Battn in 73rd Bde were attached to us for work, + joined at 4 pm. Battn found 600 men for	Ack.

Army Form C. 2118.

WAR DIARY
or
INTELLIGENCE SUMMARY.
(Erase heading not required.)

Instructions regarding War Diaries and Intelligence Summaries are contained in F. S. Regs., Part II. and the Staff Manual respectively. Title pages will be prepared in manuscript.

Place	Date	Hour	Summary of Events and Information	Remarks and references to Appendices
	27		work under X corps signals from 9pm to 5.30 Am. 2 ORs wounded. 2/Lt Mitchell joined Battn.	Ans.
MICMAC Camp	28	12 noon	Battn in camp N10 & 3.9. Same working parties.	Ans.
Nr OUDERDOM		about 1 pm.	Battn relieved by 3rd Rifle Brigade & proceeded to HUBERTUSHOEK Camp, arriving about 1 pm.	Ans.
	29	11 am	Battn left HUBERTUSHOEK Camp & proceeded to RENINGHELST SIDING to entrain for Rear Area. Arrived Siding 12.10 pm entrained at 2.20 pm.	Ans.
AFFRINQUES	30	6.25 pm	Battn arrived at LUMBRES & detrained. Marched to AFFRINQUES were Battn was billeted in farms etc.	Ans.
			Battn in billets at AFFRINQUES. Lewis Hall & 2/Lt Devlin joined Battn.	Ans.
			Casualties for month of June.	
			Officers wounded 4 killed Nil. OR's killed 25 wounded 144.	Ans.

A.D. Murphy Lieut Col
Comdg. 2nd Leinster Regt.

MEMORANDUM. No. 1.

The following Officers, N.C.Os and Privates will not go into action with the Battalion in the 1st Phase of the forthcoming operations.

1. OFFICERS.

Captain.	F.P.Hall.
Lieut.	L.S.Mathias.
2nd Lieut.	J.A.J.Nugent.
"	R.A.M.Burke.
"	P.B.Cullinan.
"	L.W.Seery.
"	P.C.Tennant.
"	R.F.Gordon.

2. OTHER RANKS. (Instructors).

No.4388.	C.S.M.	W.Puckman.		No.4579.	C.S.M.	J.Smith.
" 4797.	"	J.Hennessey.		" 9564.	Corpl.	D.Dineen.
" 7986.	Corpl.	P.O'Hare.		" 9296.	"	S.Bernardine.
" 4892.	"	C.Hogan.		" 1236.	"	T.Ferris.
		No.9564.	Corpl.	W.Hyde.		

Signallers. = 10. (to be detailed by Signalling Sergt.)
Runners. = 14.

From each Company.
    3 runners (or batmen with experience as runner.) ========= 12.

From Headquarters.
    2 runners (or batmen with experience as runners.) ========= 2.

                                                        Total. 14.

From each Company.
    1 Sergeant.
    1 Corporal.
    1 Lance Corporal.

To be detailed by O.C.Coys. (Coy instructors as far as possible).

From each Platoon.
    Two trained gunners from L.G.Section.
    One trained man from each other Section.
    (The man selected from rifle sections to be a good shot and suitable for training as a Scout.)

    In addition to the men detailed above each Lewis Gun Section will be required to leave two trained gunners at Bn.H.Q. under Sergt. Butcher to act as section reserves. The places of these men will not be filled as they are always available if required.

    The places of the men withdrawn from Lewis Gun Sections and left behind under the previous para will be filled by transferring partially trained gunners from the fourth (or carrying) platoons of Coys.

    O.C.Coys. will submit not later than to-night a nominal roll showing the N.C.Os and men to be left behind under the following headings :-

		No.per Coy.
1.	N.C.Os.	3.
2.	Runners or batmen.	3.
3.	Lewis-Gunners.	6.
4.	Rifle bombers	3.
5.	Bombers.	3.
6.	Riflemen.	3.
		21.

    Platoons will then be completed to a minimum strength of 35 other ranks by drawing on the fourth (training) platoon of Coys.
    The actual available number in each training platoon after this adjustment has been effected will then be reported to O.R.
    The following who will be employed as Signallers will not be included on platoon establishments.

"A" Coy.	No.4950.	Corpl.	T.Morris
	" 5536.	Pte.	M.Cottle
	" 5213.	"	J.Canning.

	No. 1150.	Pte.	J. Tibbenham.
	" 5566.	"	A. Kemp.
	" 10656.	"	J. Delaney.
"B" Coy.	No. 10384.	L/Corpl.	J. Boland.
	" 4270.	Pte.	M. Davis.
	" 5434.	"	A. Crouch.
	" 5432.	"	J. Clow.
	" 5428.	"	T. Bowman.
	" 5423.	"	J. Bell.
	" 10412.	"	T. Warnaby.
"C" Coy.	No. 593	Pte.	T. Jennings.
	" 5570.	"	G. Lovette.
	" 5680.	"	J. Kerr.
"D" Coy.	No. 4461.	Pte.	T. Clifford.
	" 9770.	"	E. Long.
	" 9519.	"	J. McGaughran.
	" 1648.	"	J. McGuigan.

1st June 1917.

Jos. Plowman Lieut.
Adjt. 2nd Bn. The Leinster Regiment.

2nd Battalion, The Leinster Regiment.

Circular Memorandum No. 2.

ORDERS RE CARRYING OF EQUIPMENT.
****

The equipment to be carried by each platoon is as laid down in 73 I.B. C5/2/25 (Copies of which were issued to Coys. on 29th.ult) with the following amendments:-

The ground sheet will be carried instead of the Cardigan Waistcoat.

Mess tin will be carried in the pack.

Bombs will be carried on the belt.

EQUIPMENT of PLATOONS.

Rifle Sections. (Average 1 N.C.O. and 7 men)

- (All)   200 rounds S.A.A.
- 4 men carrying shovels
- 1 man carrying pick
- 2 men carrying entrenching tool and one coil of concertina wire (the latter to be picked up at Adv.Dumps at OLD FRENCHTRENCH.)
- (4 men carrying 2 flares in pockets)

Lewis Gun Sections. (Average 1 N.C.O. and 3 men) (less scouts)

- 1 man carrying gun and revolver.
- 3 men carrying 4 magazines each.
- All   carrying 50 rounds S.A.A. and ent. tool.
- (Scouts) carry 50 rounds S.A.A. only and no additional equipment.
- (4 men carrying 2 flares in pockets).

Bombing Sections. (Average 1 N.C.O. and 7 men).

- 6 men carrying 10 bombs each and entrenching tool, and 50 rounds S.A.A
- 1 man carrying shovel and 200 rounds S.A.A.
- (4 men carrying 2 flares in pockets)

Rifle Bomb Sections. (Average 1 N.C.O. and 7 men).

- 5 men carrying 6 Rifle Grenades and entrenching tool and 150 rounds S.A.A.
- 2 men carrying shovels and 200 rounds S.A.A.

Commanders of all Sections and Platoon Sergts. carry wire cutters and 150 rounds S.A.A, also notebooks, whistles and maps (if available), a Very Pistol and 3 Very Lights of each colour (Red and Green)
(4 men carrying 2 flares in pockets)
Runners and Signallers carry 50 rounds S.A.A. only.

Platoon Flags will be carried by Platoon Runners.

On "Y" day the Commanding Officer will inspect one man of each Company equipped as laid down.

"A" Coy.	1	Rifleman.
"B" "	1	Lewis Gunner.
"C" "	1	Bomber.
"D" "	1	Rifle Bomber.

5th June 1917.

Jas Plowman
Lieut.
Adjt. 2nd Bn. The Leinster Regt.

MEMORANDUM NO 3.
P.2192.
2nd Leinster.

An Advanced Party as under will parade at 2 p.m and proceed to the Assembly Positions moving in two parties.

    2nd. Lieut J. Igoe.
    2nd. Lieut. A.J.Rowlette.
    2 Representatives from each Platoon.
    2 Representatives from Battn.Hd.Qrs.
    Pioneer Serjeant and Pioneers.
    Battalion Scouts.
    2 Runners.
    3 Signallers

The two Officers named above will report to the Adjutant, for instructions as to the work required to be done by the Advanced Party, at 12 noon.

Rations for to-morrow and full Battle Equipment are to be carried.

6th June 1917.
                Jos. Plowman Lieut.
                Adjt. 2nd Leinster Regt.

    O.C. Coys.
    Qr.Mr. (for Information)
    2nd Lieut J.Igoe.
    2nd Lieut A.J.Rowlette.
    R.S.M.

Operation Order No 15   Copy No
by
Lt Colonel A. D. Murphy M.C
Commanding 2nd Bn The Leinster Regt.

5th June 1917.

1. INTENTION

On "Z" Day the Second Army will deliver an attack on the MESSINES–WYTSCHAETE Ridge and its extension Northwards to MOUNT SORREL.

2. ACTION OF 24TH. DIVISION

The 24th Division is in General Reserve to the 9th Corps, which is on the left of the Attacking Army. After the capture of the first three objectives by the 41st, 47th and 23rd Divisions the 24th. Division will pass through the 41st Division and attack the GREEN LINE. The 73rd Brigade will attack this line on the left and the 17th. Brigade on the right.

3. PRELIMINARY MOVEMENTS

The Battalion with the remainder of the 73rd Brigade will move on Y/Z night to the Assembly Position already notified.

As soon as the situation is sufficiently developed after Zero Hour the 9th Royal Sussex Regt. and the 13th Middlesex Regt will move from their Assembly Positions to OLD FRENCH TRENCH and ECLUSE TRENCH. Liaison Officers with two runners each from "C" and "D" Coys will accompany these Battalions. The Signalling Officer will arrange for a forward Battalion Station to move with the Headquarters of 13th Middlesex Regt. and for direct communication with this Battalion during moves up and in ECLUSE TRENCH.

4. THE FIRST BOUND

The 2nd Bn Leinster Regt will move to OLD FRENCH TRENCH and ECLUSE TRENCH as soon as these trenches are vacated by the leading Battalions. "C" and "D" Coys will form the first wave and "A" and "B" Coys the second wave. If the ground permits all Companies will move in columns of half platoons in file at 50:100 yards interval but the actual disposition must depend on the nature of obstacles to be crossed and the attitude of the enemy. About 300 yards distance will be maintained between waves. Battalion Headquarters will move in rear of "B" Coy.

The positions to be occupied by Companies at the end of the First Bound are approximately:-

"C" Coy — OLD FRENCH TRENCH. (Centre of Company about its junction with trench tramway)

"D" Coy — OLD FRENCH TRENCH (Centre of Company about ARUNDEL FARM)

"A" Coy — ECLUSE TRENCH between CONVENT LANE and trench tramway

"B" Coy — ECLUSE TRENCH between trench tramway and Canal.

Batn H.Qrs. — ECLUSE TRENCH about its junction with trench tramway.

If however it is found that the hostile barrage is accurately placed on either of the above trenches the Coys will keep their Coys under as much cover as is available in artillery formation in the vicinity of the area allotted to them.

The country to be crossed on this first bound

is much intersected by hedges streams and trenches. Opportunity should be taken of the time available between Zero Hour and the time of advance for further reconnaissance but O.C. Coys themselves are not to leave their Assembly Positions without authority.

Batteries on the line of advance must be avoided as far as possible. If this is impossible the leader of the column wishing to pass through our guns must inform the Artillery Officer on duty there and ask for the guns to cease firing for the necessary period.

It is probable that only a short time will elapse between the completion of the First Bound and the commencement of the Second Bound.

5. SECOND BOUND

The Second Bound of this Battalion will be from the positions laid down in para.4. to a position of assembly about O.3. Central. This move will be ordered from Battalion Headquarters as soon as the leading Battns have cleared the German Front Line.

The disposition of Coys in the Second Bound will be as for the First Bound, but as the ground to be crossed is chiefly marsh and is in very bad condition it may be necessary for Companies to move in platoon columns. The position of Coys on completion of the Second Bound will be approximately as under:-

"C" Coy — German Front Line (Right of Coy about RUINED FARM)
"D" Coy — German Front Line (Centre of Coy about O.3.d.2.8)
"A" Coy — British Front Line South of copse O.3. Central
"B" Coy — British Front Line East of copse O.3. Central
Battn H.Q. — Western edge of copse at O.3. Central.

If the hostile barrage is severe on any of the above trenches Coys may remain short of them or go beyond them, but in no case will the advance of any Coy extend beyond the RED LINE without definite orders.

Artillery formations are to be maintained as long as possible and Companies will keep as much concentrated as the situation will allow.

6. SUBSEQUENT ACTION

The further action of the Battalion will depend on the progress of the attack on the GREEN LINE but it is probable that the next advance will be to a supporting portion in the BLACK LINE (probably about RAVINE WOOD.)

After completion of the Second Bound Coys will be prepared to take independent action as follows:-

"C" Coy — to proceed to support of 9th Royal Sussex Regt. (Battn H.Q. probably about O.10.a.1.1)

"D" Coy — to proceed to support of 13th Middlesex Regt. (Battn H.Q. probably about O.10.a.7.7.)

"B" Coy — to assist the Detachment 12th Sherwood Foresters to construct Cme trenches between the BLACK LINE and the GREEN LINE (probably about OBSCURE AVENUE (O.10.b. + d) or in O.10.c.

None of the above movements will take place without definite orders from Battn H.Q.

O.C. "C" + "D" Coys will however ensure that constant touch is maintained between themselves and the Battalion which they may be ordered to support.

7. MACHINE GUNS

One Sub-section 73rd. M.G. Coy will join the Battalion at ECLUSE TRENCH and will be attached to and will

(3)

~~will be attached~~ will move with A Company.

issued at 9.50pm   A.D. Murphy Lt Colonel
5/6/17.   Commanding 2nd Bn. The Leinster Regt

No 1. Copy   'A' Coy
   2   "   B "
   3   "   C "
   4. "   D "
   5   "   C.O.
   6   "   Adjt
   7   "   Q"m"
   8   "   R.T.O.
   9   "   R.S.M.
  10   "   H.Q. Coy.
  11   "   Intell. Officer
  12   "   Signal Officer
  13   "   Adm. Officer
  14   "   L.G. Officer
  15   "   File
  16   "   War Diary
  17   "   73 IBde
  18   "   9th Royal Sussex
  19   "   13th Middlesex

Memorandum N° 4.

P.22.10.
2nd: Leinster

In continuation of Circular Memorandum N° 2 dated 5th June 1917, every man not detailed therein to carry a pick or shovel as part of his equipment will be issued with a shovel or pick (in the proportion of 4 picks 1 shovel) at the Assembly Positions. These will be carried at least as far as the end of the Second Bound where Platoon Dumps will be formed. From this point forward it will depend on the rôle allotted to each Platoon whether these tools can be carried further or not, but the Platoon Dumps should be got forward as far as possible.

Whatever subsequent action may be ordered, Platoons will invariably advance carrying these tools, etc, detailed in Memorandum issued yesterday.

NCOs, Scouts, Signallers, Runners and N° 1s of Lewis Gun Sections will not carry tools.

6th June 1917.

Jas Plowman
Adj 2nd Bn The Leinster Regt

Copies to:
 Coys.
 Major. J. J. Freeman
 R.S.M.

Place	Date	Hour	Summary of Events and Information	Remarks and references to Appendices

WO/36

Jersey — Nom Roury of 2nd Battalion Leinster Regiment for month of July 1917

WAR DIARY or INTELLIGENCE SUMMARY

Army Form C. 2118.

July 1914. Part I.

Instructions regarding War Diaries and Intelligence Summaries are contained in F. S. Regs., Part II. and the Staff Manual respectively. Title pages will be prepared in manuscript.

(Erase heading not required.)

Place	Date	Hour	Summary of Events and Information	Remarks and references to Appendices
Affringues	1st		Bn at Affringues.	RWJ
"	2nd		Billets. Training started.	RWJ
"	3rd		Reinforcements – Officers – 0: Other ranks – 9.	RWJ
"	4th		Major Stanitzgrounds " " 1 " (Vermont)	RWJ
"	5th		2nd Lt. R.S Berry to Hospital " " 0 " 11	RWJ
"	6th		Training	RWJ
"	7th		C.S.M Murphy M.C. awarded. Sgt Sports and Smoker. Lt Col. D.S.O. Went to England on Machine Gun Course. A/Cpl Agnew v O'Brien. Pte Byrne v Morrissey. n.c.o Medal. Reinforcements – Q.R. – 11. Training	RWJ
"	8th			RWJ
LE WAST	9th		Left Billets 9.30 am and marched to LE WAST 18½ miles arriving at 4 pm.	RWJ
Affringues	10th		Lieut A.B. Hodge from Hospital. Reinforcements – Officers – 0. Other ranks – 15.	RWJ
"	11th		Return to Billets at Affringues. Left LE WAST 9.45 am arrived AFFRINGUES 4:30 am. Training.	RWJ
"	12th		Lt. M.S. Buckley to Hospital. Training.	RWJ
"	13th		C.O's Sports and Smoker. Training.	RWJ
"	14th		43rd Brigade Sports. Pries won by Bn = Cup for best all-round Regt. Jumping-Cup & Officers Jumping Cup. 100 yds & Officers Jumping Cup & Lt Blair, ? ?, 220 yds L. A. Grant.	RWJ

WAR DIARY or INTELLIGENCE SUMMARY

Army Form C. 2118.

July 1914. Part II.

Instructions regarding War Diaries and Intelligence Summaries are contained in F. S. Regs. Part II and the Staff Manual respectively. Title pages will be prepared in manuscript.

(Erase heading not required.)

Place	Date	Hour	Summary of Events and Information	Remarks and references to Appendices
Affringues	15th		Billets Affringues. Lt. A.J. McGrath to Hospital	RW
"	16th		" " } Training	RW
"	17th		" "	RW
"	18th		Left Affringues at 3.45 a.m. and marched to RENESCURE (about 13 miles) to join 11th Corps 5th Army. Arrived 11.30 a.m. Billeted for night.	RW
Renescure	19th		Left RENESCURE 5.45 a.m. and proceeded to Billets 3 miles N. of HAZEBROUCK. Arrived 9.30 a.m.	RW
Hazebrouck	19th		Billets for night.	RW
St. Sylvester- Cappel	20th		Left Billets 9 a.m. to ST. SYLVESTER CAPPEL. Arrived 10 a.m. Billets for night.	RW
32.a.2.2.	21st		Left Billets 6.40 a.m. to 32.a.2.2. Shrl 28. Arrived 10.30 a.m. 2/Lt. W. Burger to Hospital.	RW
Shrt 28.	22nd		Shots with "Russie" at " " Boxing, Jug. o. War. Last 1 round of Boxing only.	RW
N.1.A Central	23rd		Moved to N.1.A central (Sheet 28) at 6.30 p.m. Arrived 8.30 p.m. Capt. E.G. Hall to Hospital.	RW
"	24th		Officers reconnoitred route to front line.	RW
"	25th		" " assembly positions etc. Major Friend proceeded to take over command of	RW
"	26th		Reinforcements. Other ranks = 6. (13th Kinslow.	RW
"	27th		Remained in camp at N1a central. Reconnaissance of line.	RW

2353 Wt. W2344/1454 700,000 5/15 D. D. & L. A.D.S.S./Forms/C. 2118.

WAR DIARY / INTELLIGENCE SUMMARY

Army Form C. 2118.

July 1917. Part III.

Place	Date	Hour	Summary of Events and Information	Remarks and references to Appendices
Sheet 28 N.I.a central	28		In camp at N.I.a central. 2/Lt Gotting & 2/Lt Holmes joined. Three posted to "C" & "A" Coys respectively.	RW
"	29		X day. Coys left for front line in following order:- "A" Coy 2 pm, H.Q. Coy 3 pm, "D" Coy 5.30 pm, "B" Coy 7.30 pm. Batln took over from 9th Royal Sussex Regt. Relief completed 12.30 am. 2/Lt A.J. Devlin & 1 OR wounded on the way up. Capt Lambkin joined Batln.	RW
Canada Street Tunnels	30		Y day. "B" Coy in LARCH WOOD TUNNELS (Reserve Coy). "A" Coy CANADA STREET TUNNELS (Support Coy) "D" Coy mount SORREL (Right attacking Coy) "C" Coy BRITISH FRONT LINE (Left attacking Coy). Coys moved into assembly positions & no further casualties.	RW
Tunnels	31		Z day. Zero hour 3.50 am. Daylight attack. Operation Order attached. Series of Objectives attained. 2/Lt A. Dundas joined Batln. Officer casualties in action.	RW
			Killed:- Lieut A.D. Hodge (3rd Lin R.) 2/Lt A.N. Pender (4th B.R.) 2/Lt E. Quinlan (5th Lin R.) 2/Lt P.E. Tremant (3rd B.R.) 2/Lt N.J. Smith (4th Lin R.) 2/Lt R.A.M. Burke (3rd B.R.) Died of Wounds:- Lieut W.J. Porter (Lin R.) 2/Lt A. Pritchett (B. Lin R.) Wounded:- Capt C. Craddock (6 Lin R.) Capt J. Blackman (on duty Lin R.) Lieut R.H. Hoye	RW RW

July 1917. Part IV.

WAR DIARY
INTELLIGENCE SUMMARY.

Place	Date	Hour	Summary of Events and Information	Remarks and references to Appendices
			(4th L.R.) 2/Lt W.H. Osborne (4th Lin R.) 2/Lt M.C.L. Sharpe (Lin R.) 2/Lt A.J. Rostlett (4th L.R.) 2/Lt R. Dunphy (3rd Lin R.) 2/Lt J. Agar (4th Lin R.) 2/Lt J.H. Lennon (5th Lin R.)	ex
			Officers O.R. Killed 6 28 Wounded 9 149 Missing - 53 Died of Wounds 2 -	enn
	3/8/17		A. Murphy Lt Col. Comdg. 2/Leinster Regt.	

INSTRUCTIONS FOR COMPANIES.   P.3736.

(N.B. Each Company has only two fighting Platoons).

To be distributed to :-
    COMPANY COMMANDERS.
    PLATOON COMMANDERS.
    PLATOON SERGEANTS.
    COMPANY SERGT.MAJORS.
    and made known to all ranks.

1. ASSAULTING COMPANIES.   ('D' Coy. on RIGHT).
                            ('C' Coy. on LEFT).

(a) The task of your Company is the capture of that portion of both 1st and 2nd objectives allotted to the Battalion: Company frontage 120 yards increasing to 250 yards at the 2nd objective. Advance on a narrow front (i.e. two sections) distributed in depth. Interval between men 6 yards increasing to 8 yards when the first objective is reached.

(b) Keep close touch with the advance of the Companies on right and left and keep close under barrage which begins to move at Zero + 4. Not to be diverted by small opposition or by side shows which will be dealt with by 'moppers up', but proceed straight through under barrage (100 yards in 4 minutes) to 1st objective. Constantly check direction and watch Sun and obvious landmarks. Report progress of self and others constantly. When barrage lifts off first objective at Zero + 33 assault and capture. At once push out scouts under new protective barrage (200 yards in front) and reorganise Company and consolidate. Check direction, memorize country, estimate ranges, watch flanks, and look out for immediate counter-attack. About 40 minutes to be spent here. Report situation and see how others on flanks have got on. At about Zero + 65 get both lines out under barrage parrellel to new objective (this means a slight right incline).

(c) Your next objective has nearly twice as long a frontage as the first. Get your second wave echeloned on your outer flank, so that as you advance you can keep extending your front without changing direction or intervals. The right hand man of the leading line of 'C' Company is responsible for direction and should have been given a point to march on (which all his Section must know). At Zero + 75 advance under barrage, filling up the gap on your outer flank as it appears, by using as many sections as necessary of your 2nd Platoon (who are echeloned on that flank). Keep close up to barrage at same pace as before. Watch adjoining Coys during movement and frequently check direction. Do not be led away by others who may be wrong themselves. When barrage lifts off 2nd objective at Zero + 99, assault and capture.

Immediately push out covering party and scouts, get touch with Companies on right and left, and commence consolidation. All men not out in front covering can work, but rifles must be handy and equipment on. A firing position for every man is the first essential, then wire, then good parapets and cover from shell fire. Mobile patrols as well as covering party must be sent out in front as soon as our barrage permits to ascertain action of enemy. Report situation and draw your position on map. Light flares when aeroplane comes over and wave platoon flags. REMEMBER Mutual support with other Units.

(d) When 2nd objective is definately secured, reform in depth, and look out for counter-attack. See if you have enough S.A.A. Bombs, Rifle Grenades, etc, and if they are properly distributed.

2. SUPPORTING COMPANY. ('A' Coy).

(a) Your task is to keep in touch with the advance of the Assaulting Companies and to help them if necessary, but not to get in their way. By means of your 'mopping up' platoon you will prevent them from being distracted from their true objectives by minor opposition, and you will deal with sudden emergencies from flanks or from dug-outs they have passed. Keep in touch with both front Companies and with both flanks throughout. (If you can see them, watch them; if you cannot see them push out a file or two until touch is maintained).
Mopping up sections are to be very mobile patrols and are not tied down to distance or interval. If they see enemy showing fight, they will go to them and kill them, following on after the front Companies as soon as each job is done. If the enemy surrender they will hunt them back to our lines (no escort required) where they will be collected by a party specially detailed. Each mopping up section is working by itself, and when its work is done it is to follow on to the rendezvous previously arranged by the Company Commander.

(b) The supporting platoon follows the leading Companies, helps them with covering fire and reinforces them if necessary. Must not be diverted from its task by the 'moppers up' who will be prowling about round them and whom they will probably have to pass through.

(c) Unless help is asked for, the supporting sections will not close up on the leading Companies, but will remain in Artillery Formation at a convenient distance in rear of the 1st objective.

(3).

(d) When the advance to the 2nd objective commences at Zero + 75 mopping up sections follow the leading lines and act as before. When their work is done whey will assemble at a place previously arranged between the two objectives and remain in support to the leading Companies. If help is required, the Platoon Commander will give it and notify O.C. 'A' Coy. and Battalion Headquarters.

(e) The supporting platoon will proceed to a suitable line slightly in front of the first objective, and will consolidate and occupy two Strong Points covering both flanks (Approximate position J.25.b.60.00. and J.25.b.70.40). From these points keep in touch with front line, assist them with covering fire or by other means, and constantly report situation. Give them help if they call for it and report that you have done so.

3. RESERVE COMPANY ('B' Coy).

(a) Your duty is to act as general reserve to the Battalion. If more opposition is encountered by the three leading Companies than is expected, you may be required to assist to clear up any difficult situation and so enable the objectives to be gained. If such action is necessary (which is not likely) you will act as a complete Unit or by Platoons, and you will not (unless in very exceptional circumstances) be employed to reinforce other Companies.

(b) As soon as the hostile barrage permits after Zero hour, you will be moved from your assembly positions in Artillery Formation to the vicinity of our old front line where you will discover and keep in touch with the situation on front and flanks by means of small patrols and connecting posts. Report the situation to Battalion Headquarters and notify your own position. Look out for landmarks and points of direction to help you when you have to advance. Watch what hostile barrage is doing, as it is likely to remain fairly constant.

(c) As soon as the advance to the 2nd objective has begun (about Zero + 85) you will advance in Artillery Formation to a convenient position clear of barrage, near the captured BLUE LINE (1st objective). Keep in touch with front Companies throughout advance. Select most suitable position for defence of high ground about BLUE LINE, and consolidate 3 or 4 STRONG Points covering Battalion front, and supporting front Companies, and 'A' Companies STRONG POINTS. Wire your strong points and

(4)

make them as strong as possible. This is the REAL line of resistance, and you can give covering fire to everyone else.

Estimate ranges, memorize country, get touch on flanks, report situation and your own position and progress. See if front Companies want anything and give them all you can spare (i.e. S.A.A., Bombs, Water etc) and send back for more. If all has gone well, you will be required to co-operate (about Zero + 6½ hours) with the advance of the 17th Brigade on our left, on the GREEN LINE. Your task is to fill the gap between the centre of our line (where there is a salient) and the right of the GREEN LINE (Rifle Brigade), and to prevent their flank (which is far more advanced than ours) being turned. To do this effectively you must establish three Strong Points in the gap (which is about 560 yards). The gap is across a valley, so each Strong Point will be able to see those on its flanks, and can maintain communication. Frequent patrolling between Strong Points by night will be necessary, as you will be some way in front of our captured line (Your left Strong Point will be about 450 yards in front of the BLACK LINE) but you will be well supported by 'C' and 'D' Companies, and by the 17th Brigade on the high ground behind you and on your flanks.

(D) After you have taken up this new position and have so gained touch between the two Brigades, our other Company will be re-organised so that a new reserve is available in case of any new development.

4. POSITION OF BATTALION HEADQUARTERS.

Battalion Headquarters which will first be established at CANADA STREET TUNNELS (I.30.a.80.30) will move to about the centre of the BLUE LINE (about J.25.b.2.2) when the advance on the 2nd objective commences.

A. O'M Murphy Lieut Colonel,
Commanding, 2nd.Bn.The Leinster Regt.

Ref. Sheet. 1/10,000 ZILLEBEKE.   Copy No........

OPERATION ORDERS No. 27.
by
Lieut Colonel A.D.MURPHY, D.S.O., M.C.
Commanding 2nd.Battalion, The Leinster Regiment.
26th JULY, 1917.

****

1. INTENTION.

(a) The 24th Division will co-operate in the forthcoming operations which will commence on ZERO DAY, at an hour to be notified. The 24th Division is the right attacking Division of the II Corps of the Fifth Army. The 30th Division are on our left and the 41st Division of the Xth Corps are on our right.

(b) The 73rd Brigade is the centre attacking Brigade of the 24th Division. The 17th Brigade is on our left and the 72nd Brigade on our right.

(c) The battalion is the left assaulting Battalion of the 73rd Brigade. The 7th Northamptonshire Regiment is the right assaulting Battalion, and the 13th Middlesex Regiment are in Brigade reserve.

2. OBJECTIVES.

The objectives of the Battalion are :-

(a) The capture and consolidation of the BLUE LINE.
(b) The capture and consolidation of the BLACK LINE.
(c) The extension of our new front to the left, in order to maintain touch with the right of the 17th Brigade, after the capture of the GREEN LINE.

3. PRELIMINARY DISPOSITIONS AND ACTION OF COMPANIES.

Before ZERO HOUR on ZERO DAY Companies will be disposed in or near our present front line, in the formations already explained to Companies. The preliminary dispositions and the action of Companies in each of the three different phases of the attack, is explained in detail in "Instructions for Companies" which has already been issued.

4. BOUNDARIES.

The boundaries between Companies are as under :-

IN THE BLUE LINE.

LOWER STAR POST is inclusive to "B" Company.
The point of junction of Companies will be about J.25.b.25.15.

IN THE BLACK LINE.

The STRONG POINT about J.26.a.40.60. is inclusive to "B" Coy.
The point of junction of Companies will be about J.26.a.33.10.

The boundaries between Battalions and Brigades are shown on the SPECIAL MAP issued to O.C. Companies.

5. ARTILLERY BARRAGE.

The general action of the Artillery Barrage will be as under :-

(a) At ZERO HOUR the barrage will be put down 200 yards in front of the ASSEMBLY POSITION. At ZERO + 4 it will commence to move forward at the average rate of 100 yards in 4 minutes until it reaches the BLUE LINE on which it will pile up.

(b) At ZERO + 22 minutes, it will lift off the BLUE LINE and advance at a similar rate as before until it forms a protective barrage 200 yards in front of the BLUE LINE, where it will stop until ZERO + 83 minutes.

(c) At ZERO + 83 minutes the barrage will advance again at the rate of 100 yards in 4 minutes until it reaches the BLACK LINE on which it will pile up.

(d) At ZERO + 99 minutes it will lift off the BLACK LINE and advance at a similar rate as before until it forms a protective barrage 200-300 yards in front of the BLACK LINE, where it will stop until ZERO + 140 minutes.

(e) At Zero + 140 the barrage will move forward again until it forms a new protective barrage about 400-500 yards in front of the BLACK LINE where it will remain. (This latter lift is to enable the leading Companies to push patrols well forward).

The barrage timings for Brigades on either flank are slightly different, and men must be warned not to be misled by them.

At ZERO + 6 hours and 28 minutes, the advance on the GREEN LINE by the 17th Brigade under a new barrage will begin.

6. FLARES.

"C" and "D" Companies will light FLARES (in groups of three) when called upon by the Contact Aeroplane, at about the following hours :-

    (a) Zero + 1 hour. (BLUE LINE).
    (b) Zero + 2 hours and 30 minutes. (BLACK LINE).
    (c) Zero + 6 hours.
    (d) Zero + 9 hours.

Every man will carry one flare, but only the most advanced line of the Battalion will light flares when called upon.

Contact Aeroplanes will be marked by two Black Plates fixed to the rear of the planes.

The call for flares is a succession of "A's" on a KLAXON HORN. If this fails to produce an answer, the aeroplane will fire a WHITE LIGHT as a further call.

7. CONSOLIDATION and STRONG POINTS.

After the capture of the BLUE LINE and during the reorganisation of the Platoons :-

"C" and "D" Companies will push forward covering parties under our protective barrage, and will commence the consolidation of one or more STRONG POINTS each at the most suitable position in the ground gained. "A" Company will dig themselves in Supporting Positions in rear of the BLUE LINE.

When the advance from the BLUE LINE commences, the supporting Platoon of "A" Company will establish TWO STRONG POINTS approximately at J.25.b.70.50. and J.25.b.65.85. and will consolidate these as supporting points to the BLACK LINE. The garrison of each STRONG POINT will be about two sections, and the NORTHERN one (J.25.b.70.50) -which is the MOST IMPORTANT - will have a sub-section 73rd M.G. Company to assist the garrison. Touch between these two STRONG POINTS will be maintained by small connecting posts. Arrangements will be made for covering fire to support the Companies in the BLACK LINE and Units on the flanks.

After the capture of the BLACK LINE, "C" and "D" Companies will again push forward small covering parties under our protective barrage, and will consolidate the ground gained, by a series of small Strong Points sited so as to obtain the best possible field of fire. Intervals between posts will be watched by small connecting posts.

The "Mopping up" Platoon of "A" Company will assemble in a suitable supporting position to be notified previously by O.C. "A" Company, and will dig themselves in.

(3)

"B" Company will continue the consolidation of the BLUE LINE on the lines previously started by "C" and "D" Companies, and will be prepared to take over the STRONG POINTS at J.25.b.70.50. and J.25.b.65.05. in the event of the former garrison being ordered forward to reinforce the front line.

At Zero + 140 (when our barrage lifts to a line 400-500 yards in front of the BLACK LINE) the leading Companies will each push forward one section and establish posts at the following approximate positions :-

        "D" Company ---- J.26.a.60.66.
        "C" Company ---- J.26.a.75.40.

8. PRISONERS OF WAR.

A Prisoners' Collecting Station will be established at about I.30.b.70.15. as soon as possible after Zero Hour. This will be under the command of the Battn. Provost Sergeant, who will be responsible for the collection of prisoners, and for the provision of escorts to conduct prisoners to the DIVSL. CAGE at H.31.d.5.1. He will obtain a receipt for all prisoners handed over, and will keep a record of the numbers sent down.

Prisoners captured by Companies will be collected into batches and sent back to the BATTALION COLLECTING STATION under small escort. Slightly wounded men and men returning with messages are to be used for escort duty as far as possible.

9. MEDICAL.

The BATTALION AID POST will be at CANADA STREET TUNNELS close to Battalion Headquarters. "Walking wounded" will proceed direct to the Divisional Collecting Post at LARCH WOOD TUNNEL.

Stretcher cases will be collected by the Battalion Stretcher Bearers as soon as possible and will be carried to the Battalion Aid Post.

In no case will any Officer, N.C.O. or man withdraw from the fighting area for the purpose of conducting wounded to the rear.

10. LIAISON.

Throughout the operations all Commanders will keep the closest liaison with Platoons or Companies on their flanks.

The following Battalion Liaison Officers are detailed :-
    2/Lieut W.L.M.NEWNHAM---- with the three attacking
    battalions of the 17th Brigade.
    (1st Royal Fusiliers, 12th Royal Fusiliers, 3rd Rifle Bde)

    2/Lieut R.O'N.BUTLER with the 7th Northamptonshire Regt.

Battalion Liaison Officers will be responsible for keeping the Battalion to which they are attached informed of the plans of, and the situation on the front of their own Battalion - and vice versa. They will report to their own Battalion Headquarters at least every 3 hours to obtain the latest information.

11. DUMPS.

The main BATTALION DUMP of S.A.A., Bombs, Tools, R.E.Material, etc, will be at CANADA STREET TUNNELS (Battn.Hd.Qrs). Two smaller Dumps will be established before Zero, near the assembly trenches.

After the capture of the BLACK LINE, two advanced dumps will be formed in the BLUE LINE --one at LOWER STAR POST and one at about J.25.b.30.40. O.C. "B" Company will be responsible for forming these and for keeping them replenished.

(4)

12. MAINTAINING TOUCH WITH ENEMY.

As it is possible that the enemy may decide to withdraw beyond the area actually attacked, O.C. Companies will ensure by means of energetic patrols that the ground to our front is searched as far forward as our barrage will permit, and that touch with the enemy is maintained.

13. ACTION OF VICKERS GUN.

(a) One sub-section 73rd M.G.Company under 2/Lieut CARTER, will be under the orders of O.C. "A" Company, and will move with them to the STRONG POINT about J.25.b.70.50. In the vicinity of which, positions for M.G's will be selected and emplacements made so as to support the defence of the BLACK LINE and to assist the further advance of the 17th Brigade on the GREEN LINE.

An N.C.O. and runner of the 73rd M.G.Company will accompany "C" Company to the first objective to reconnoitre and select the best position for these guns. The further action of these sub-section will be at the discretion of O.C. "A" Company.

(b) One sub-section 73rd M.G.Company under 2/Lieut BLOWER will be under the orders of O.C. "B" Company and will move with them to the BLUE LINE. During the 3rd phase this sub-section will advance with "B" Company and will co-operate with them in the extension of our front to connect with the 17th Brigade.

14. COMMUNICATIONS.

The Signalling Officer will arrange for a Battalion Report Centre to be established in rear of Assembly Trenches (about I.30.b.90.20.) This report centre will be in communication with Battn.Hd.Qrs. by telephone and Visual, and by a relay system of runners. During the 1st phase all messages will be sent by runner to Battn.Hd.Qrs. through the Report Centre. After the capture of the BLUE LINE, an advanced Brigade Forward Station will be established at J.25.d.4.9. and all messages during the 2nd phase should be passed through this Report Centre.

In addition, relay stations with exchanges will be established at I.30.b.7.7. and J.25.d.0.0. and a Visual Receiving Station on the forward slope of MT.SORREL. Report centres will be marked by a BLUE and WHITE FLAG, and by a BLUE LAMP at night. Relay Station will be marked by a WHITE FLAG with a BLUE "R" on it.

All urgent messages will be sent in open envelopes so that Transmitting Officers may use their discretion as to the method of transmission.

15. OBSERVATION POSTS.

The Battalion Intelligence Officer will be at the Battalion Report Centre from before Zero hour until after the capture of the BLUE LINE. He will submit frequent reports of the situation to Battn.Hd.Qrs.

After capture of the BLUE LINE a Battn.O.P. (1.N.C.O. and 3 men) will be established just NORTH of LOWER STAR POST. This O.P. will continue to be manned throughout the operations of the Battalion, and frequent reports of the situation and action of the enemy will be sent. Periodically, Battn. Scouts will be sent forward to obtain definite information and to make detailed reconnaissances.

16. BATTALION HEADQUARTERS.

BATTALION HEADQUARTERS will be established on "Y" DAY at CANADA STREET TUNNELS (I.30.a.80.30)

After the advance on the BLACK LINE has commenced, Battalion Headquarters will be established at LOWER STAR POST (about J.25.b.20.10).

Lieut Colonel,
Comdg.2nd.Bn.The Leinster Regiment.

Copy No. 1. O.C."A" Coy.
"   "   2. O.C. "B" "
"   "   3. O.C. "C" "
"   "   4. O.C. "D" "
"   "   5. Commanding Officer.
"   "   6. 2nd In Command.
"   "   7. Adjutant.
"   "   8. Regt.Transport Officer.
"   "   9. Quartermaster.
"   " 10. Medical Officer.
"   " 11. Battn.Intelligence Officer.
"   " 12. Battn.Signalling Officer.
"   " 13. Battn.Bombing Officer.
"   " 14. 2/Lieut W.E.W.NEWENHAM.
"   " 15. 2/Lieut.R.O'M.BUTLER.
"   " 16. Regtl.Sergt.Major.
"   " 17. Regtl.Provost Sergt.
"   " 18. 73rd Infantry Bde.
"   " 19. 17th Infantry Bde.
"   " 20. 7th Bn.Northamptonshire Regt.
"   " 21. 13th Middlesex Regt.
"   " 22. 73rd M.G.Coy.
"   " 23. War Diary.
"   " 24. File.
"   " 25. 9th Royal Sussex Regt.
"   " 26. 73rd L.T.M.Bty.
"   " 27. O.C."B"Coy.,13th Middlesex Regt.

ADDENDA to
OPERATION ORDERS. NO.27.

Action of Supporting Company, 13th MIDDLESEX REGIMENT.—

1. The Supporting Company of the 13th Middlesex Regiment under Capt. DOVE will move from its Assembly Positions in such time as to reach the following positions by ZERO + 1½ hours.

   (a) Company (less 1 Platoon) CANADA STREET TUNNELS. (Vacated by "B" Company 2nd Leinsters).

   (b) One Platoon to the concrete dug-outs in the Front Line (about I.30.b.85.35).

2. The further action of this Company will depend on the situation but will probably be as follows.—

   (a) In the event of the reserve Company of the 2nd Leinster Regiment being required to assist the attack on the BLACK LINE or to repel a counter-attack, the Middlesex Supporting Company will receive orders to move to the BLUE LINE to be in general reserve, and to continue the consolidation of this line.

   (b) In the event of heavy casualties or serious opposition which would involve the use of the Leinster Reserve Company in the 1st or 2nd phase of the attack, the Middlesex Supporting Company may receive orders to carry out or to support the 3rd phase, i.e. The extension of our front to connect with the 17th Brigade.

   (c) In the event of the failure of Units on either Flank, the Middlesex Supporting Company may receive orders to form a defensive flank with our portion of the BLACK LINE facing either NORTH or SOUTH.

   (d) In the event of a shortage of S.A.A., Bombs, R.E. Material, etc., after the capture of the BLACK LINE, the Middlesex Supporting Company may be ordered to provide small carrying parties to convey these to the front line or to replenish advanced dumps in the BLUE LINE.

3. Most careful reconnaissances by all Officers and Sergts. of the Company is essential, and all Commanders will be expected to be able to find their way quickly to any stated point on the 2nd Leinster Regiments' front, or to any stated unit of that Battalion at any time throughout the operations.

All ranks of the Middlesex Supporting Company are to be thoroughly well acquainted with the dispositions and details of operations of the 2nd Leinster Regiment.

Lieut Colonel,
Comdg. 2nd.Bn. The Leinster Regiment.

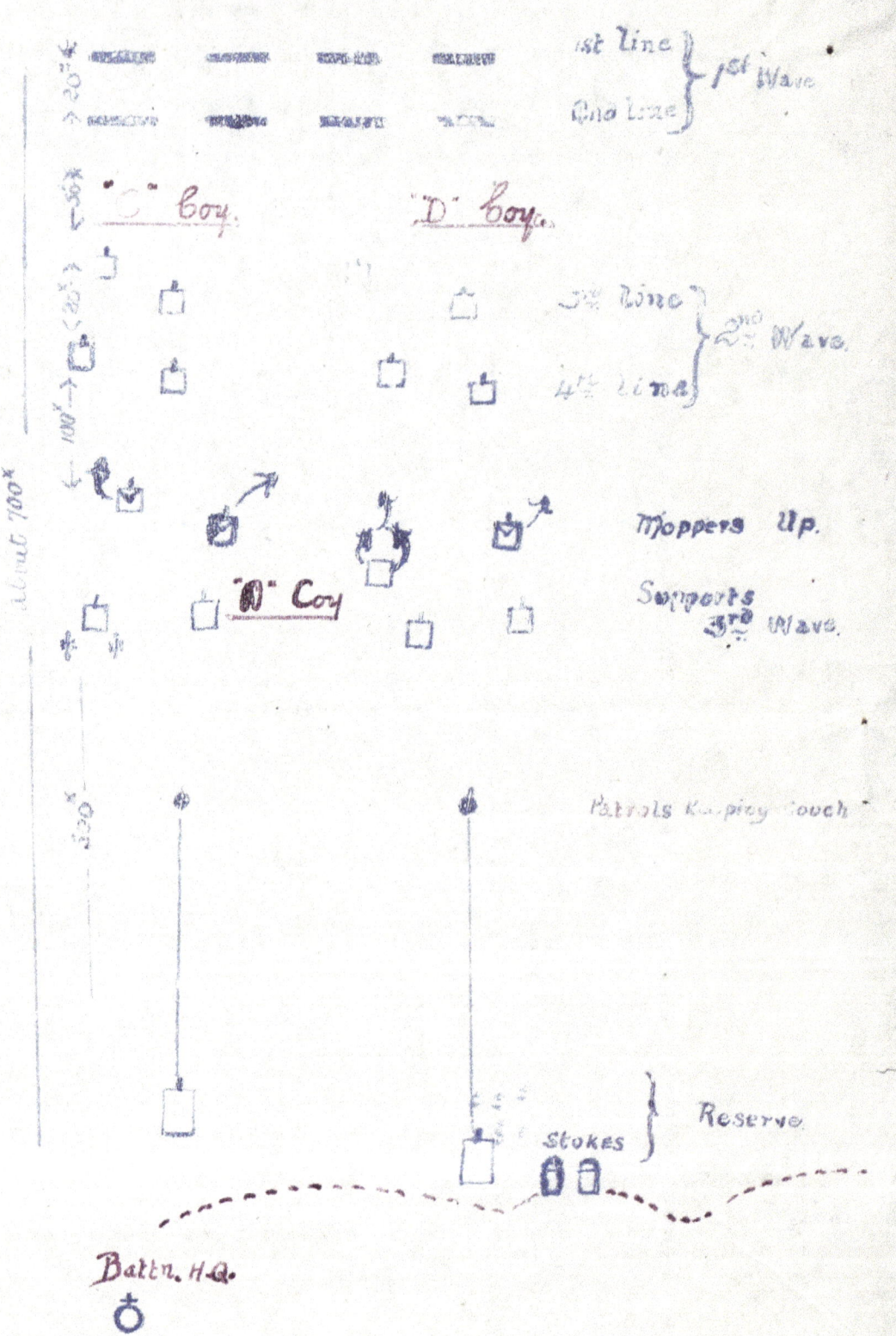

2nd Position
(After capture of 1st Objective)

                                                                    1st Wave
                                                                    Consolidating and
                                                                    reforming.

    'C' Coy.   'D' Coy.
                                                                    2nd Wave
                                                                    Possibly some of
                                                                    1st Wave used
                                                                    to reinforce

About 700'

                                                                    Moppers Up.
                                                                    Searching ground
              'A' Coy.
                                                                    This 3rd Wave
                                                                    passing through
                                                                    Moppers Up.

                                                                    Patrols expiring
                                                                    ??? and reporting
                                                                    situation

                                                                    Reserve ready to
                                                                    advance if required
                            Signals.

    Batt. H.Q.   Batn H.Q ready
                                                                    to advance.

2nd Objective

3rd Position (Approaching 2nd Objective)

C Coy   D Coy

Note gradual extension of line to cover both flanks

"A" Coy

Moppers Up finished work forming Supporting line

New S.P.   New S.P.

Supporting Platoon Consolidating S.Ps.

B Coy

Objective

Bn HQ

CIRCULAR MEMORANDUM No.2.
****

The following will be the Personnel to be left behind (in accordance with Para XXX "Training of Divisions for Offensive Action"), and the duties for which they are responsible.

Major J.R.FREND (to accompany the Battalion to the Assembly positions and to be in charge of all Administrative arrangements).

Capt. N. ALGEO.	"D" Coy)	Company Commanders
Lieut L.S.MATHIAS.	"B" ")	and 2nd in Commands.
Lieut R.H.HAYES	"A" ")	(Administrative Coy Duties).
2/Lieut W.E.W.NEWENHAM	"C" ")	
2/Lieut J.A.J.NUGENT	"A" "	(i/c "Echelon B" personnel).
2/Lieut R.A.M.BURKE	"A" "	(Actg R.T.O.)
2/Lieut A.MITCHELL	"B" "	(Platoon Comdr. II Corps Reinforcement Depot.)
2/Lieut P.B.CULLINAN	"B" "	(II Army School)
2/Lieut R.E.GORDON	"B" "	(G.H.Q., L.G.Course)
2/Lieut L.W.SEERY	"C" "	(Reserve Officer)
2/Lieut R.A.MOORE	"C" "	(II Army Bombing Course)
2/Lieut R.O'N Butler	"D" "	(Bn.Liaison Officer)
2/Lieut R.N.HALL.	"D" "	(Stokes Gun Course)

N.C.O's. COMPANY SERGEANT MAJORS.   (2)

    8694. C.S.M. BRADLEY.   (Furlough)
    3338. C.S.M. BUCKMAN.   (Hospital).

SIGNALLERS.   (10)

    (be detailed by Signalling Officer).
        (Nominal Rolls to be forwarded forthwith to Orderly Room)

RUNNERS.   (13)
  (or Batmen)

    (2 to be detailed by each Coy, and 5 by Bn.H.Q.)
        (Nominal Rolls to be forwarded to Orderly Room forthwith)

GAS INSTRUCTOR.
    9296. Cpl BERNADINI.

BOMBING INSTRUCTOR.
    4982. Cpl. HOGAN.

LEWIS GUN INSTRUCTORS.
    7986. Cpl.O'HARE.
    1236. Cpl. FERRIS.

OTHER INSTRUCTORS.
    7390. Sergt. BARNWELL.
    9564. Cpl. DINEEN.
    9444. L/Sgt. BOYER.

OTHER N.C.O's.

SERGEANTS.

        3990. Mc'EVOY.
        8408. HILL.
        2429. BYRNE.
        9867. WILLIAMS.

CORPORALS.

        6061 Cranston
        ~~1236. FERRIS.~~
(L/Sgt) 9010. BYRNE.
        1036. HYDE.
        5500. WICKENS.

Lance-CORPORALS.

        7744. NOLAN.
        9885. WEBB.
        1813. YOUNG.
        3114. MORRISSEY.

and 1 Private per Section to be detailed by O.C. Coys.

(Nominal rolls to be forwarded to Ord. Room forthwith)

Lieut Colonel,
Commanding, 2nd.Bn. The Leinster Regiment.

O.C. Coys.
Major J.R.FREND.
Signalling Officer.
Bombing Officer.
Lewis Gun Officer.

CIRCULAR MEMORANDUM No.3.

All EXTRA EQUIPMENT for the forthcoming operations is being drawn this morning and will be issued to Companies as soon as received.

O.C. Companies will arrange for the Re-Issue to Platoons in accordance with instructions already issued.

The Commanding Officer will inspect the Companies in their FULL FIGHTING EQUIPMENT this evening at the following hours :-

"D" Company .... 5 p.m.
"C" Company .... 5.30 p.m.
"A" Company .... 6 p.m.
"B" Company .... 6.30 p.m.

After inspection extra equipment will be collected within Platoons and the equipment of each Platoon seperately, will be conveyed by Battalion Transport tomorrow morning to a point as far forward as possible on the route to Assembly Positions; here it will be stacked in Platoon Dumps and picked up by Platoons as they pass.

Each Platoon will detail one man to accompany the Limbers in the morning, and to remain in charge of Platoon Equipment till it is drawn by men of His Platoon.

Rations for consumption on "Z" DAY will be dumped with Platoon Equipment.

The result of above arrangements will be that each man arrives in his Assembly Position tomorrow night with his complete FIGHTING EQUIPMENT on him, and with his rations for "Z" DAY in his pack.

This equipment and these rations will be kept intact till "Z" DAY.

Rations for the period between arrival in Assembly Positions and ZERO DAY will be brought up seperately under the usual arrangements.

28/7/17.
R.W.Warren
2/Lieut,
A/Adjt. 2nd. Leinster Regiment.

Copy to :- O.C. Companies.
Major F.F.FREEMAN.
R.T.O.
QUARTERMASTER.
R.S.M.

OPERATION ORDERS No.28.
by
Lieut Colonel A.D.MURPHY, D.S.O., M.C.
Commanding 2nd.Battalion, The Leinster Regiment.
29th JULY 1917.

1. The Battalion will relieve "A" and "C" Companies of the 9th Royal Sussex Regiment in the line to-night.

2. Movement from Camp will be by Platoons at 200 yards interval as far as VOORMEZEELE. From VOORMEZEELE to Brigade Headquarters LARCH WOOD by Sections at 400 yards interval.
   Leading Section of Companies will pass Brigade Headquarters at:-

   "A" Company......... 6 p.m.
   "D" Company .... 9 p.m.
   "C" Company......... 9.30 p.m.
   "B" Company .... 11.30 p.m.

   The leading Platoon of each Company will leave Camp at the following times:-
   "A" Company......... 2 p.m.
   H.Q. Company......... 3 p.m.
   "D" Company......... 5 p.m.
   "C" Company......... 5.30 p.m.
   "B" Company......... 7.30 p.m.

3. The Lewis Gun Limbers and limbers with Fighting Equipment will accompany the leading Section of their respective Companies.

4. Officers Kits and Mess Stores will be carried to Q.M.Stores by Officers servants.

R.Warren
2/Lieut,
A/Adjt, 2nd Leinster Regiment.

Ref. Operation Orders No. 28. Para 4.

Officers kits will be left in the present Camp and stored under arrangements to be made by the Regtl. Quartermaster Sergeant.

R.W. 2/Lieut.
A/Adjt. 2nd. Leinster Regiment.

OPERATION ORDERS. No.29.
by
Lieut Colonel A.D.MURPHY, D.S.O.,M.C.
Commanding 2nd. Battalion, The Leinster Regiment.
30th JULY,1917.

1. ZERO HOUR to-morrow will be at 3.50 a.m.
 The three leading Companies will be disposed in their final Assembly Positions by 3 a.m.

2. As the enemy barrage generally becomes more intense about 2 a.m. it seems advisable for Companies to move to the forward Assembly Positions between midnight and 2 a.m.

3. If conditions are favourable Companies will therefore leave their present positions at the following hours :-
 "D" Company.........,12 midnight.
 "A" Company.........,12.30 a.m.

 If O.C."D" Company decides to delay his departure on account of hostile barrage, he will notify O.C."A" Company who will also postpone his accordingly.

4. A considerable time must be allowed for getting men out of tunnels and dug-outs and for checking equipment etc.

5. Movement to the front line will be by sections at small intervals via, SAP F. and the path running SOUTH of ILLUSIVE SUPPORT to the centre of Battalion front.
 All Commanders will carefully reconnoitre this approach before it is quite dark.

6. Before leaving present front line after ZERO HOUR, O.C. "B" Company will draw from BRIGADE DUMP there, additional sandbags, concertina wire and S.A.A. (in bandoliers) and convey these to the BLUE LINE when he moves there

 Sd. R.E.WARNER,2/Lt for Lt.Col,
 Comdg. 2nd. Bn. The Leinster Regiment.

Copy to O.C. Coys.
 " " Intelligence Officer.

Ref. Para 3. The exact hour of departure from present positions are left to the discretion of Company Commanders. The timings given therein are to be considered only as suggestions.

 Sd. R.E.WARNER 2/Lieut,
 A/Adjt. 2nd Bn. The Leinster Regiment.

NARRATIVE of OPERATIONS undertaken by 2nd Battalion, The
LEINSTER REGIMENT on the 31st JULY, 1917.

****

1. ASSEMBLY.

The night of 30/31 JULY was normal as regards hostile Artillery activity. The enemy kept up a slow fire continuously throughout the night and periodically a short intense barrage was placed between our front line and the forward slopes of Mt.SORREL. During the early part of the night a white tape was run out from CANADA TUNNEL straight across country to the left of our ASSEMBLY POSITIONS and another tape was laid parallel to our first objective, to assist the leading Companies in their deployment.

About mid-night the leading Companies left their tunnels and dug-outs in the forward area and moved by Sections to their previously arranged ASSEMBLY POSITIONS in the vicinity of our front line. This early assembly was decided on as it had been observed that the hostile bombardment on back areas usually increased in violence about 2 a.m.

The three leading Companies were in their ASSEMBLY POSITION by 3 a.m. and the code word "A" was sent to BDE.HEADQUARTERS. Less than 10 casualties were obtained during assembly.

The RESERVE COMPANY was at 3 a.m. moving forward from LARCH WOOD TUNNEL.

2. ACTION OF THE THREE LEADING COMPANIES.

At ZERO HOUR (3.50 a.m.) our barrage came down and the leading wave closed up on the barrage. It was then very dark. The hostile barrage was very quick in response and came down on our front line and vicinity almost immediately. It lengthened to MT.SORREL and CANADA STREET about ZERO + 10 minutes.

As soon as our barrage permitted, the three leading Coys. pushed forward as arranged, but the darkness and the wide extension of the leading two lines made it very difficult to keep touch.

A few of the enemy were encountered lying in shell holes less than 100 yards from our front line, but these offered no resistance, and surrendered freely.

The first opposition met was at the hostile front trench about ILIAD RESERVE and ILLUSIVE RESERVE where there was some fighting, a few Germans being killed and about 20 prisoners taken. After about 5 minutes delay, our Companies then pushed forward towards their first objective.

(2)

The ground to be crossed was extremely muddy and was much broken up by our heavy preliminary bombardments. It was found that the pace of the barrage was much too quick and our men were unable to keep up to it from the start.

The enemy's main line of resistance was in LOWER STAR POST and on the ridge running NORTH and SOUTH of this. This high ground was strongly garrisoned, and the well concealed and well protected fire positions here provided a clear sweep of fire for their garrison down the valley along which the right Company of the Battalion had to advance.

A few minutes after ZERO HOUR the right of the advance came under a very heavy M.G. and Rifle fire from this ridge and from LOWER STAR POST itself, and many casualties were caused. All the Officers of this Company fell and only one Sergeant remained. To avoid this fire-swept valley the survivors seemed to have turned Northwards and crossed the high ground on their left, so joining in with the left Company who were themselves suffering severely from enfilade and frontal M.G. and Rifle fire. Similarly on the extreme right flank of the Battalion the effect of this hostile fire from the LOWER STAR positions was to turn the 7th NORTHAMPTONSHIRE REGT. to their right so as to avoid the same valley. An Officer and about twelve men of my Battn. accompanied them.

By the time the left of the advance reached the Western edge of the wood North of LOWER STAR POST casualties had [been] very severe, and only isolated groups of men were availab[le to] push on to the assault of the enemy trenches in front of th[e] BLUE LINE. The left of the Battalion was now in touch with 17th BRIGADE, and the survivors of the three leading Companies were collected and organised for a further advance in conjunct[ion] with the 1st ROYAL FUSILIERS. Our barrage at this time was out of sight, the wood was thickly wired with low trellis wire which was quite intact, and the enemy were resisting strongly from a group of loopholed concrete dug-outs in the BLUE LINE. After much delay, and after several unsuccessfu[l] efforts made by small parties in a most gallant manner had added considerably to the list of casualties, these dug-outs were eventually carried by a double flanking movement, and we obtained possession of the enemy trench.

We were now practically in possession of the BLUE LINE, and in touch with the 17th BRIGADE, but a large gap existed on the right flank and it was impossible to clear this up without reinforcement of men, ammunition and bombs.

Consolidation of the captured line was commenced and it was decided not to make any further advance. Enemy fire was still very active from the front and from the right flank, but a patrol was pushed out to try to get touch on the right and to collect any stragglers. This patrol did not return

3. ACTION OF THE RESERVE COMPANY.

The Reserve Company had orders to move in Artillery Formation direct from LARCH WOOD TUNNEL to the vicinity of our old front line and to follow the advance from that point as far as the BLUE LINE. The Company reached a point 200 yards in advance of our front line before 6 a.m. and were fired on from the high ground about LOWER STAR POINT. Deployment was ordered and as large numbers of the enemy could be observed on the ridge to the right front, the men were got into a fire positions and engaged the enemy across the valley at about 550 yards range. A Vickers Gun and a Stokes Gun were also brought into action here.

It was obvious that the enemy were still in possession of a large portion of the ridge and that it was impossible to advance further without serious casualties. The Company was therefore ordered to consolidate a position about ILIAD RESERVE, and to engage the enemy with fire until it could be ascertained where the flanks of the leading Companies of the Battalion and the left flank of the Northamptonshire Regt. rested.

During the morning an enemy aeroplane flying very low apparently observed the new position of the Reserve Company and soon a severe bombardment was opened which grew in intensity and caused many casualties. Although slight movement to either flanks and forward were made to avoid this devastating fire, nevertheless by 12 noon the Company had suffered casualties exceeding 50%.

Throughout the whole morning and afternoon the enemy maintained an almost continuous heavy bombardment on our old front line and an area 300 yards on each side of it. This made communication and the evacuation of the wounded extremely difficult.

About 1 p.m. the situation in the front line was fairly clear and it had been ascertained that a gap of about 400 yards existed in the BLUE LINE between the right of the Battalion and the left of the Northamptonshire Regt. In order to fill this gap the Supporting Company of the Middlesex Regt. was ordered forward at 3.15 p.m. This Company however was weak and had already given up one Platoon to gain touch between the Reserve Company at ILIAD RESERVE and the Supporting Battalion of the

17th Brigade near the embankment at J.25.a.6.6.

The Supporting Company of 13th Middlesex Regt. moved to our front line via the 17th Brigade area, reaching there about 6.30pm. They extended the right flank of the front line about 100 yards. and formed a defensive flank facing SOUTH.

The situation during the night remained as above as the relieving Companies of the 13th Middlesex got lost in the darkness and failed to reach the front line until about 6 a.m., 1st August.

4. GENERAL REMARKS.

As requested I attach the following remarks :-

(a) BARRAGE.

There is little doubt that the pace of our barrage was, considering the heavy state of the ground, the darkness, and the amount of undamaged wire in the woods, much too fast. From the start the men state they were quite unable to keep near the barrage, and when they were approaching the BLUE LINE the barrage seemed to have passed right on towards the BLACK LINE. It appears to have been at least two hours after ZERO hour when the BLUE LINE was actually captured.

(b) HOUR OF ZERO.

ZERO HOUR was much too early. It was quite dark when the advance began, and the points of direction previously selected for Companies were invisable. Touch was difficult to maintain as the men were intentionally widely extended, and even the direction of the barrage could not be clearly observed in the darkness.

(c) HOSTILE RESISTANCE.

The enemy's advanced troops did not cause very much trouble, but, his main line of resistance on the top of the ridge was very resolutely defended. I do not think that the resisting power of well sited concrete dug-outs loopholed for fire in three directions has been previously recognised. Some of these were quite undamaged by our bombardment and were the cause of the majority of our casualties in the advance.

(d) EQUIPMENT.

In my opinion the men are still too heavily laden. A good number of bombs and Rifle Grenades are necessary, but I should prefer to see the majority of these carried by supporting Companies rather than by the men constituting the first and second lines of an attack. For the latter, the bayonet, the Lewis Gun and plenty of ammunition are the most important requirements. I would suggest that only one days rations is carried and that the iron ration is dumped near Battn. Hd.Qrs. as a "Barrage Ration" to be sent up in case of emergency only.

(6)

(e) AEROPLANE PHOTOS and MAPS.

The supply of these was very good, but I would suggest that important features and objects such as emplacements, dug-outs etc be clearly marked on Aeroplane Photos by the specially trained Intelligence Staffs before they reach Battalions. This proceedure would call the attention of Battalion Commanders to points of interest on their front which otherwise might very easily be missed.
A large number of photographs and maps reached Battalions of xxxxxxx areas which do not concern them, and these only waste time and tend to confuse.

(f) BARRAGE RATIONS.

The experiment of a "Barrage Ration" is little use. The supply of rations and water is organised within Battns. on a system which starts at the Battalion Transport Lines. There is a very distinct danger of having no carrying party to bring a barrage ration to the front line.
I suggest that dumping of the iron ration only, as a barrage ration.

(g) WOUNDED.

The system of evacuation of wounded leaves much to be desired. Battalion Medical Officers and bearers did all that was possible, but a more comprehensive system of searching and clearing the forward area by large parties under definate supervision is badly needed. The carrying of wounded in these last operations proved a most difficult and tedious job, and though large numbers of bearers were available in the areas between our own front line and Battn. Hd.Qrs. the hardest work of clearing the captured line and its vicinity under heavy shell and M.G.fire fell almost entirely on the Battalion bearers whose numbers are quite inadequate for the work. I suggest that in future operations — especially in bad weather — a special party of bearers under supervision of an officer be allotted to each Battalion or Brigade to assist in clearing the wounded from the most advanced positions.

(h) MARKING TRENCHES and TRACKS.

The enormous value of marking out with white tape and notice boards, tracks and trenches for traffic during the action and afterwards has not been always appreciated.

It should be possible to run a white tape from Ba[ttn]
to the most advanced captured line shortly after Zero,
and this would be invaluable for runners, carrying parti[es]
and relieving units.

Relieving parties and carrying parties cannot expect
reliable guides on the first day of an attack. The guides
know little more than any one else, and Officers and N.C.Os
in charge of parties going to the front line must be
prepared to find their own way by means of maps and
compasses.

(i) COMMUNICATION.

Our communications throughout were unsatisfactory
and companies were entirely dependent on runners who at
times could ill be spared. In my Battalion three
signallers went forward with each Company for Visual duties
but I am convinced that this was too many and is likely
to cause a serious shortage of signallers at a later stage
when they will be badly needed.

If both Battn.Hd.Qrs. and Bde.Hd.Qrs. had been moved
further forward before ZERO HOUR, the difficulty of
communication would have been much simplified.

(j) COUNTER BATTERY FIRE.

Judging from the heavy barrage which the enemy put
down in the vicinity of our old front and support lines
shortly after Zero Hour, and from the way this barrage
increased in intensity and was kept up during the whole
of Z day, it appears that our counter battery work was
disappointing.

(k) MORALE.

These operations have clearly proved that the fighting
value of one man in a cheerful mood is worth that of many
who are miserable and depressed. The extremely bad weather
following the day of the attack might have had a serious
effect on the men's morale and the wisdom of postponing
operations and of carrying out reliefs was apparent.
I would suggest that in future operations in this country --
--ing view of the possibility of sudden bad weather --
supplies of dry clothing, waterproofs, and waders be kept

Army Form C. 2118.

WAR DIARY
INTELLIGENCE SUMMARY.
(Erase heading not required.)

Instructions regarding War Diaries and Intelligence Summaries are contained in F. S. Regs., Part II. and the Staff Manual respectively. Title pages will be prepared in manuscript.

WO 37

Place	Date	Hour	Summary of Events and Information	Remarks and references to Appendices
Secret			2nd Battalion The Scottish Regiment for the month of August 1914.	

Army Form C. 2118.

WAR DIARY
or
INTELLIGENCE SUMMARY.
(Erase heading not required.)

Instructions regarding War Diaries and Intelligence Summaries are contained in F.S. Regs., Part II. and the Staff Manual respectively. Title pages will be prepared in manuscript.

Place	Date	Hour	Summary of Events and Information	Remarks and references to Appendices
Shrewsbury Forest.	1/9/17.		Holding line. LOWER STAR POST after zero hour relieved by 13. Middlesex Regt + returned to camp near Dickebusch — arriving about 12 noon —	App 1
Dickebusch Camp.	2.3.4. 5.6.7.		Camp at Dickebusch.	App 2
"	8.9.		Ordered to proceed to Trenches in relief 13th Inf/. Lot Regt. B"4" left Camp at 3.30 p.m. relief was completed en route & handed to B"4" returned to own Camp.	
do.	9/9/17. 8. 9. 10.		Remained in Camp — Capt. C.C. Barry M.C. + 22 O.R. joined Batt. 7th. 8. 17. —	App 3
Canada Tks.	11.12.13.14.		Proceeded to CANADA TUNNELS near SHREWSBURY FORREST. Both our line relief completion 6 A.M. 2 O.R. killed during relief. Holding above line. Casualties. Capt. P.S. LAMBKIN. gassed., 3 O.R. Killed + 15 O.R. wounded.	App 4
	15.16.17. 13.14.15.17.		Relieved by 9th E. Surreys of proceeded to Camp A. MICMACK arrived.	App 5
MICMACK CAMP.	14 P/17.		6.15 A.M. Casualties on relief. 2 O.R. wounded. Capt N. AIGE 0 wounded buried in duty. —	App 6

2353 Wt. W.2344/1454 700,000 5/15 D.D. & L. A.D.S.S./Forms/C. 2118.

Army Form C. 2118.

WAR DIARY
or
INTELLIGENCE SUMMARY.

(Erase heading not required.)

Instructions regarding War Diaries and Intelligence Summaries are contained in F. S. Regs., Part II. and the Staff Manual respectively. Title pages will be prepared in manuscript.

Place	Date	Hour	Summary of Events and Information	Remarks and references to Appendices
Camp A.	15.8.17 to 20.8.17		In Camp. Training 4 hours daily. 20 m.m. employed on making an ASSAULT Course. 2/Lt John 8 7th Bn. & 6 officers from 9th Bn. joined at 4 p.m. received 125 Regt of Grenadiers in Camp. J. at back about	
MICKMAC	21.8.17		Remained in Camp J. DICKEBUSH.	
DICKEBUSH	22.8.17			
Do.				
CANADA TUNNELS	23.8.17 26.8.17		also men relieved the 8th Buffs in CANADA TUNNELS on taking over the Front Line in SHREWSBURY FOREST. A very quiet tour. Artillery on casualty, mine shelling, on enemy patrols & heavy bombs. Which resulted in the following casualties. 2/Lt. J. J. Naylor killed, 1 O.R. killed 24 O.R. wounded. — 12 Bty Reinforcements 1725. joined us in Camp — B'ln arrived at MICMAC Camp about 6 A.M.	
MICMAC CAMP A.	27.8.17 28.8.17		Training & general clean up. Do. men company arranged etc.	
	29.8.17			
	30.8.17		Found working parties for Cable laying LARCH WOOD. Training —	
	31.8.17		Left A Camp. at 8.30 p.m. en rout to Camp near DICKEBUSH. where Bn was transferred	

5353 Wt. W. 23541/1454 700,000 5/15 D.D. & L.   A.D.S.S./Forms/C. 2118.

2nd. BATTALION, THE LEINSTER REGIMENT.

HONOURS and REWARDS
awarded during the month of AUGUST, 1917.

THE DISTINGUISHED SERVICE ORDER

Lieut-Colonel A. D. MURPHY, M.C.

THE DISTINGUISHED CONDUCT MEDAL.

2887. Sgt. J. DELANEY.
4240. L/Cpl. M. McGUIRE.
584.   "   E. JONES.

THE MILITARY MEDAL.

9051. Sgt. H.A. HOWES.
7277. "   J. KAVANAGH.
8029. L/Sgt. C. LYALL.
4504. Cpl. N. RIELLY.
5423. "   E. LAMB.
7608. Pte.(L/Cpl) M. DONOGHUE.
4985. Pte. W. DUFFY.
4436. "   P. CLINTON.
9916. "   J. COONEY. (S.B.)
7596. "   T. BYRNE.
9017. "   R. BYRNE.
1212. "   F. BAES.

Army Form C. 2118.

WAR DIARY

INTELLIGENCE SUMMARY.

(Erase heading not required.)

Instructions regarding War Diaries and Intelligence Summaries are contained in F. S. Regs., Part II. and the Staff Manual respectively. Title pages will be prepared in manuscript.

VK 38

Place	Date	Hour	Summary of Events and Information	Remarks and references to Appendices
Secret.			2nd Bn. Leinster Regiment for the month of September 1917.	

WAR DIARY or INTELLIGENCE SUMMARY

Army Form C. 2118.

Place	Date	Hour	Summary of Events and Information	Remarks and references to Appendices
DICKEBUSH.	1.9.17.		Battalion in Camp "L". DICKEBUSH. Church Parade. all Ranks. 1.9.17. 11 AM	
do.	2.9.17.		do. " " 2 hours Training Daily – Work continued on Bomb SHELTER WALLS round BIVOUACS.	
TRENCHES INVERNESS COPSE.	3.9.17.		Battalion relieved the 7th WILTS REGT at INVERNESS COPSE about 3 p.m. (Operation order No 32 attached) Relief Compte. 4.25pm (one casualty) Our ARTILLERY active on back areas. QUIET NIGHT. Capt. Ploughman & 2/Lt Brierley acting Military Cross.	
do.	4.9.17.		In trenches – Hostile aircraft very active during the day. Hostile artillery very active on back areas. on the 4th the B.Q.C provided around the line.	
	5.9.17		2/Lt Moon. G.W. & C.A.N. Holden joined.	
	6.9.17		B" relieved in trenches by the 8th R.W. Kents. commencing about 10am & B"i company.	
CAMP A MICMAC.	7.9.17	10 AM	to Camp A. MICMAC. relief completed by 2.50 pm – 8. O.R. Joined. 2/Lt J.A. Wheatley, J.A. Stainton, 2/Lt J.A. Brierley J.A.	(3)
do.	8.9.17.		Camp A. Training & general cleaning up. Working parties 1 neo & 25 men J.J. Shelley & 18 O.R. joined. Company Training	
do.	9.9.17.		Camp A. Church parades – Range Practices carried out – and Inspections.	
do.	10.9.17.		Camp A. General training, C.O.s inspection Company	
H CAMP DICKEBUSH.	11.9.17.		B" in Camp H. left Camp A. 10.30 A.M. arrived camp H. 12 noon –	
do.	12.9.17.		CAMP H. Coy parades. training from 9 to 12 noon –	

WAR DIARY or INTELLIGENCE SUMMARY

Army Form C. 2118.

(Erase heading not required.)

Place	Date	Hour	Summary of Events and Information	Remarks and references to Appendices
CAMP H. DICKEBUSH.	13.9.17.	12 noon	Bttn moves to HALLEBAST CROSS ROADS CAMP. The Bttn completed this day its 3rd year in FRANCE. A list of Officers, W.O.s NCOs & Men who disembarked with the Bttn & are serving with it is attached. See published Battalion Orders attached.	4. 5
HALLEBAST Cross Roads Camp.	13.9.17.	3 pm	Bttn arrived, complete pitching Camp.	
do.	14.9.17.	10.30 am	Battalion C/P. marching to WESTOUTRE.	6, 6A.
WESTOUTRE	14.9.17.	4.40 pm	Bttn reached Camp WESTOUTRE, work pitching Camp.	
BERQUIN BILLET AREA.	15.9.17.	6 am.	Bttn marched to route between OUTERDOM - RENINGHELST, where it embussed at 8 am & disembussed at 9.15 am at OULSTEENE BERQUIN AREA. At 11.45 am it marched to Billet AREA.	
do.	16.9.17.		Company Training - do under Specialists	
do.	17.9.17.		The G.O.C. 24th Division inspected the Bn at 11.15 am & conversed by Bn. marching past in Column of Route. General Rouchin & Brig. provides were carried out afterwards. Capt. J. Plough made an eye on the monthly Special Leave.	
do.	18.9.17		Company Training & Specialist Classes. Lewis Gun Teams were practised on the Range.	

WAR DIARY or INTELLIGENCE SUMMARY

Army Form C. 2118.

(Erase heading not required.)

Place	Date	Hour	Summary of Events and Information	Remarks and references to Appendices
BERQUIN Billet AREA.	19.9.17		Training under Coy arrangement & Specialist Classes. 2nd. Lieut. A. Murphy 2nd/O. N.F. rejoined the battalion from Command of 73rd Bde. and assumed command.	
By RAIL	20.9.17		Bn. Entrained at Bailleul Main Station 10.25 AM, & detrained at 5:30 p.m. at BAPAUME. 33 O.R. joined at BARASTRE CAMP.	7.
BARASTRE CAMP.	21.9.17		BAPAUME & marched to BARASTRE CAMP. 2/Lieuts A. Murphy & J.O. proceeded to BAPAUME STATION for detraining duties, remainder Bn. general cleaning up parades under Coy arrangements.	8, 9, 10.
Do.	22.9.17		Commanding officers inspection all Companies, Coy parades & Specialists.	2
Do.	23.9.17		Church parade. C.O. Coy Cmdrs & I.O. proceeded & reconnoitred new area to be taken over by Brigade. & proceeded by Bus, as far as TEMPLEUX. (6.2.b. Sheet 62.C.).	
HAUT-ALLAINES, Camp. (C.29.B.5.B)	24.9.17		Bn. moved from BARASTRE CAMP 9.40 AM marching to HAUT-ALLAINES, and arrived there 1.30 p.m. Parades, Bathing all Companies, P.T. & P.D. for those who fell out during the march, period 2 hours.	
HANCOURT.	25.9.17		Bn. left HAUT-ALLAINES 8.30 AM, 50% proceeding by Bus, at that hour 10.40 AM, the remainder by Bn. left moving by Route, Bus party reached HANCOURT 1.30 p.m. — party by Route arrived 3 p.m.	

WAR DIARY or INTELLIGENCE SUMMARY

Army Form C. 2118.

Instructions regarding War Diaries and Intelligence Summaries are contained in F.S. Regs., Part II. and the Staff Manual respectively. Title pages will be prepared in manuscript.

(Erase heading not required.)

Place	Date	Hour	Summary of Events and Information	Remarks and references to Appendices
HANCOURT	26.9.17	5pm 26.9.17	Battalion (less details) proceeded from Billets to Line (Brigade Reserve) Route Roisel, HARGINCOURT. Details marched to Camp at K.25.a.i.i. Shellions with band, leaving HANCOURT at 6.30 p.m., arriving at destination about 7.30 p.m. Transport remained at HANCOURT.	
LINE	27.9.17		Bttn in Brigade Reserve in dug outs.	
Detail Camp	27.9.17		Details carried out programme of work, & Specialist training, Lewis Gun & N.C.O. classes.	App. 11.
LINE	28.9.17		Bttn in Brigade Reserve. 40 men on carrying fatigue 9th Royal Army at 7.30 p.m. 10 men to 93rd Bde.	
Detail Camp	28.9.17		Parades as previous day.	
LINE	29.9.17		Bttn in Brigade Reserve. Carrying parties, 40 men 9th Royal Irish at 7.30 p.m, 40 men 1st W.Yorks, 10 min 23rd Bde.	
Detail Camp	29.9.17		Parades as previous day. 2nd Lt. P.B. Cullinan attd. OR. Proceeded to set Camps. 2nd Lt. W.E. Newenham & 1 O.R. to Coy Commander Course at III Army School 2nd Lt. G.A. Moore & 2 O.R. to Sniper's course, III Army School Com. Off: admitted to hospital 11 a.m. Medical officer inspected details & transports proceeded to Reinforcements promoted on this tour -	
LINE	30.9.17		Bttn in Brigade Reserve. Working parties as 29th. MAJOR J.R. FRENO proceeded to England on 14 days leave. Capt. S.P. Hall rejoined Bttn from Hospital. Divine service in line R.C. 9 am. C. of E. 9.30 am.	
DETAIL CAMP	30.9.17		Two hours Specialist training. Divine Service R.C. 10.30 a.m, C.of E. 12 noon. The re-arrangement of DETAIL CAMP was carried out under Rd: orders at 2 p.m.	

W. Newenham 2nd Lt
2nd i/c Regt.

G.D Murphy Col
Comdg 2nd Leinster Regt.

Army Form C. 2118.

WAR DIARY
INTELLIGENCE SUMMARY.
(Erase heading not required.)

Vol 39

2nd Battalion Leinster Regiment
for the month of
October 1917.

Army Form C. 2118.

WAR DIARY
or
INTELLIGENCE SUMMARY.
(Erase heading not required.)

Instructions regarding War Diaries and Intelligence Summaries are contained in F. S. Regs., Part II. and the Staff Manual respectively. Title pages will be prepared in manuscript.

Place	Date	Hour	Summary of Events and Information	Remarks and references to Appendices
October 1917.				
HARGICOURT.	1st		In bivouacs at L.10.a. in Brigade Reserve. Working parties for the front line.	Rlw.
"	2nd		ditto.	Rlw.
"	3rd		ditto.	Rlw.
"			Freeman a/r for senior officers course at Limpfield Aldershot.	Major S.L.
Front Line	4th	5 pm.	Batt. relieved the 7th Northamptonshire Regt the right coy of the 9th Royal Sussex Regt in the right sub section of the Brigade sector. Y.1.D.6.3 to E.30.e.90.25 (I.B.S. 87).	Rlw.
"			Relief completed by 9.30 pm. 8 ORs joined the Batt.	
"	5th		Front line. Lt & QMr. H.O. Lazier wounded. Enemy extremely quiet.	Rlw.
"	6th		Whole time came into force at 1 AM. 2nd Lt. ditto.	Rlw.
"	7th		Front line. Enemy very quiet.	Rlw.
"	8th	5pm.	Relieved by the 7th Northamptonshire Regt. Became Batt. in support at L.10.a. Relief completed by 2pm. 2nd Lt. J. Houlston joined the Batt.	Rlw.
HARGICOURT.	9th		In Brigade Support. The Batt. found the usual front line working parties.	Rlw.
"	10th		ditto.	Rlw.
"	11th		ditto.	Rlw.
			was admitted to hospital, accidentally injured.	2/Lt A. Dunlar

Army Form C. 2118.

WAR DIARY
or
INTELLIGENCE SUMMARY.

(Erase heading not required.)

Place	Date	Hour	Summary of Events and Information	Remarks and references to Appendices
J.K. (con't)	12th		Bn Brigade Support. Usual Working Parties found. Capt J Morrow granted leave daily at home.	RW
HARRICOURT	13th		ditto.	RW
"	14th	5 pm	The Battn relieved the 7th Northamptons Regt in the front line. Relief completed at 11 pm.	RW
Front Line	15th		2/Lt L.J. McSpadden & 2/Lt P.H. Holden rejoined Battn from Lt troops behind. More joined the Battn. Enemy slightly more active.	RW
"	16th		ditto. Major J.R. Sand rejoined from leave.	RW
"	17th		Front line. Enemy quiet. Capt A. H.B. Guvulty joined the Battn.	RW
"	18th		Front line. Enemy quiet. The Battn took over new front line to the left, and handed over a portion of the right to the 2nd Bn Royal Berks Regt. New Battn front line runs from B.1.6.40.35 to F.30.c.85.90. Battn HQ establishes temporarily at SLAG HEAP L.28.d.55.15.	RW
"	19th		Front line. Enemy quiet.	RW
"	20th	5 pm	The Battn was relieved by the 7th Northamptons & proceeded to billets in HERVILLY.	RW
HERVILLY	21st		Battn in Divisional Reserve. Training and Working Parties for the R.E.s usual. Area Commandant on improving billets etc. 26 OR's joined the Battn.	RW
"	22nd		Battn in Div Reserve. Training. Working Parties as usual.	RW

Army Form C. 2118.

WAR DIARY
or
INTELLIGENCE SUMMARY.
(Erase heading not required.)

Instructions regarding War Diaries and Intelligence Summaries are contained in F. S. Regs., Part II. and the Staff Manual respectively. Title pages will be prepared in manuscript.

Place	Date	Hour	Summary of Events and Information	Remarks and references to Appendices
Oct. (cont)				
HERVILLY	23rd		Bath in Divisional Reserve. Training thinking parties as usual.	RW
"	24th		Ditto. A Brigade Tactical scheme was carried out from	RW
"	25th	9am to 12.30 p.m. Batts in Divisional Reserve. Training thinking parties as usual. 2/Lt A.G. Appleyard, 2/Lt T.J. Burphy, 2/Lt A. Woods & 2/Lt P.R. Grenville joined the Batt. 9 O.R's joined the Batt.	RW
"	26th	2.30pm	The Batt. left for VRAIGNES in accordance with new scheme of holding the Divisional front with 2 Brigades in the line than in Reserve. The move was cancelled en route & the Batt. returned to HERVILLY arriving at 6pm. 2/Lt E.G. McLeish & 2/Lt G.L. Appleyard were admitted to hospital sick.	RW
"	27th	2.30pm	The Batt. relieved the 7th Northumps in the front line, and had Coys in unit at TEMPLEUX-LE-GUÉRARD. Relief complete by 8pm. New Batt. HQ established at L.5.b.3.2	RW
Front Line	28th		In front line. Enemy rather more active. Lots with machine guns & artillery. Capt J.H. Barrow wounded. 2/Lt W.G. Russell joined the Batt. Day fairly quiet. Enemy less active. 2/Lt W.G. Formey admitted to hospital sick	RW
"	29th			RW

Army Form C. 2118.

WAR DIARY
or
INTELLIGENCE SUMMARY.
(Erase heading not required.)

Place	Date	Hour	Summary of Events and Information	Remarks and references to Appendices
Trenches (cont)	30th		Batts. in front line. Enemy quiet.	Russ. Rlw.
	31st		Batts. in front line. Relief company relieves at 6.30 A.M. Enemy quiet.	Rlw.
			Casualties for the month.	
			2 Officers wounded, 1 OR killed, 7 ORs wounded.	
			Presentation of Medal Ribbons.	
			The undermentioned W.O's, NCOs and men of the Batt. were presented with their medal ribbons by Lieut General Sir W.P. Pulteney, K.C.B., K.C.M.G., D.S.O., Comdg. III Corps, on 13th October 1917.	
			No. 7677 RSM. Smith M.C.	
			No. 12240 L/C McClune D.C.M.	
			" 8694 B.S.M. Bradley M.M.	
			" 7277 & 9115 Kavanagh M.M.	
			" 8029 Sgt. Lyall M.M.	
			- 4504 Cpl. Reilly M.M.	
			No. 7608 L/C Donoghue M.M.	
			" 4228 Pte. Hanlon M.M.	
			" 1212 Pte. Baes M.M.	
			A.G Murphy Lieut Col.	AnS.
			Comdg. 2nd Leinster Regt.	

WAR DIARY

INTELLIGENCE SUMMARY.
(Erase heading not required.)

2nd. Battalion The Leinster Regiment

For the month of

November 1914.

Place	Date	Hour	Summary of Events and Information	Remarks and references to Appendices

Army Form C. 2118

WAR DIARY
or
INTELLIGENCE SUMMARY.
(Erase heading not required.)

2nd Bn. The Lincolnshire Regt.

Place	Date	Hour	Summary of Events and Information	Remarks and references to Appendices
November 1914.				
Fort Lois	1st		Bn in Fort Lois (Right Sub sector) Nothing unusual. Enemy very quiet.	PAC
"	2nd		"	PAC
"	3rd		Relieved by 9th Bn Northamptonshire Regt. and moved to Brigade Support as under.	PAC
			A & B Coys at L.10.d. (under command of Major J. R. Hind)	
			C & D Coys at TEMPLEUX QUARRIES	
TEMPLEUX	4th		Brigade Support	PAC
"	5th		"	PAC
"	6th		Heavy hostile shelling of TEMPLEUX QUARRIES commenced about 11.30 am until 12.30 pm extremely accurate. Lt Col Murphy DSO MC, Lieut Eastman, ADS, Wilcke & Ke Brar & RSM Capt Warner and Lt GA Moore were in HQH Mess attempt to lowerdess admire shell stopped report on their meals, killing the CO, MO, and 6 OR, and mortally wounding Lt GA Moore. Capt Warner escaping with a wound on both arms - the only survivor. Shelling was kept up at intervals of 50 minutes throughout the day the night. Capt JE Hind assumed command of Bn at 1.15pm and arrived QRH 6.2am. Lt J McCallnan took over duties of a/c Adjt at 2pm.	PAC
	7th		Funeral of Col ROISEL CEMETERY at 2.30 pm. attended by BGC, GOC and Capt Edw.	PAC

Army Form C. 2118.

WAR DIARY
or
INTELLIGENCE SUMMARY.
(Erase heading not required.)

1st/4th Northampton Regt.

Place	Date	Hour	Summary of Events and Information	Remarks and references to Appendices
November 1917				
TEMPLEUX	8th		Bn Brigade Support. Bn HQrs; A & B Coys at L10a. C & D Coys, Quarries.	9MC
	9th		Bn relieved 1st Northamptonshire Regt. in the right sub sector.	PMC
HARGICOURT	10th		Bn in front line. Nothing unusual. Enemy quiet.	PMC
Templeux	11th		"	PMC
"	12th		"	
"	13th		"	PMC
"	14th		"	
"	15th		Bn relieved by 1st Northamptonshire Regt and proceeded to HERVILLY as Divisional Reserve.	PMC
HERVILLY	16th		Bn while in Bn employed on Working Parties except 12 men of B Coy and 1st Russell and 12 men of C Coy under 2nd Words under Capt C.C.Burroughs who were practising for raid.	PMC
"	17th		"	PMC
"	18th		"	
"	19th		"	PMC
"	20th		Raiding parties of 2 officers and 24 O.R. proceeded to HARGICOURT by lorries at 10.30 p.m. Advanced GHQ HQrs established by Major J.C. Laird and adjutant. Capt C.C. Burroughs and 2nd Philby O/C Scouts Parties.	PMC

Army Form C. 2118

WAR DIARY
or
INTELLIGENCE SUMMARY.
(Erase heading not required.)

Instructions regarding War Diaries and Intelligence Summaries are contained in F.S. Regs., Part II. and the Staff Manual respectively. Title pages will be prepared in manuscript.

Place	Date	Hour	Summary of Events and Information	Remarks and references to Appendices
November	1917			
HERMIES.	21st	5.55 a.m.	Raid at 5.55 a.m. very successful but no live prisoners. Enemy on approach immediately fled, when our party entered his trench. Several torn fom dead Bosches furnished the necessary identification. Material damage inflicted. 1 dug out blown up and a trench store Casualties inflicted on enemy. Our Casualties 2/Lt Purcell and 2 other ranks slightly wounded 1 O.R. killed. 1 other rank (?) believed killed.	PAC PAC PAC PAC PAC
HARGICOURT	22nd		Bn relieved 1st Northamptonshire Reg.t in the front line (Right Sub sector)	PAC
"	23rd		Bn in the line. Enemy quiet. Fighting patrols in No Mans Land. nothing to report	PAC
"	24th		"	PAC
"	25th		Major L.R. Rand appointed Lt. Col. Lieut D.M°Cann N.C. appointed Captain.	PAC
"	26th		Attempted raid by enemy of 1 officer and 12 O.R. repulsed by bombs and machine gun fire at 6.70 a.m. Casualties 5 O.R. wounded.	PAC
"	27th		Bn relieved by 4th Northamptonshire Reg.t and moves to Brigade Reserve "A" & "B" at L.10.a. under Capt. G.G. Grenfell. Bn H.Q.rs and C.I.D.Q.rs at TEMPLEUX QUARRIES in METROPOLITAN TUNNELS.	PAC

Army Form C. 2118.

WAR DIARY
or
INTELLIGENCE SUMMARY.
(Erase heading not required.)

Instructions regarding War Diaries and Intelligence Summaries are contained in F. S. Regs., Part II. and the Staff Manual respectively. Title pages will be prepared in manuscript.

1st Bn Staffordshire Regt

Place	Date	Hour	Summary of Events and Information	Remarks and references to Appendices
	1917			
TEMPLEUX	28th		Bn in support. Usual working parties.	P&C
"	29th		" " " "	P&C
"	30th		Preparing for move to HAUT ALLAINES on the 12th next. Heavy shelling of SCOTS QUARRIES started at 6.30 this morning. Before HQ' runners had time to realize what was happening one dropped right in their midst killing one and wounding five Cpl Alps wounded at 12.30 p.m. later 6 HAUT ALLAINES prepared. Killed all coming from direction of NUIROY, 500 shells predominating. 2Lt Johnson and Sutton to 7th Corps Infantry School. On standing by to fire assistance to 55th Divison in case of necessity.	P&C
			Casualties during November	
			1st, 1 O.R. wounded 9th 1 Other rank wounded	P&C
			2nd 1 " " " 10th 2 " " "	P&C
			6th 2 Officers killed (C.O. & M.O.) 11th 1 " " "	P&C
			2 wounded (I.O. & Adj) 14th 2 " " Mount Relieves killed	P&C
			6 Other ranks killed 20th 2Lt W.L. Arnold Downes	P&C
			7 " " wounded mount 2Lt Appleyard wounded (accidental)	P&C
			1 Other rank killed. 1 Other rank mound Relieves killed D.	P&C

WAR DIARY or INTELLIGENCE SUMMARY

Army Form C. 2118.

Place	Date	Hour	Summary of Events and Information	Remarks and references to Appendices
	November 1917		Casualties during month.	
	20th		3 other ranks wounded. / 30th Capt Alpes wounded	PBC
	21st		1 " " " / 1 O.R. killed	PBC
	23rd		5 " " killed / 5 wounded	PBC
	26th		5 " " wounded	
	30th		Capt M Alpes wounded 1 other rank killed 5 other ranks wounded	PBC
			Reinforcements during month.	PBC
	3rd		Lieut R.S. Holmes from Hopital	
	5th		2 O.R. joined from Corps Reinforcement Camps 2/Lt J.S. Appleyard from Hopital	PBC
	9th		1 " "	PBC
	11th		2/Lt W Howell joined.	PBC
	18th		S.C. Bates, 2/Lt E. W Terry and 25 other ranks joined from Corps R. Camp	PBC
			Total casualties during Month.	
			Officers killed. Officers wounded. Other ranks killed. Other ranks wounded	PBC
			3 4 13 29	
			Reinforcements Officers. Other ranks.	
			5. 28.	

J. R. French. Lt.Col.
Commanding 1st London Rifles

Army Form C. 2118.

WAR DIARY
INTELLIGENCE SUMMARY
(Erase heading not required.)

War Diary of the 2nd Battalion The Leinster Regiment for the month of November 1917

Vol 41

Army Form C. 2118.

WAR DIARY
or
INTELLIGENCE SUMMARY.
(Erase heading not required.)

December 1917.

Instructions regarding War Diaries and Intelligence Summaries are contained in F. S. Regs, Part II. and the Staff Manual respectively. Title pages will be prepared in manuscript.

Place	Date	Hour	Summary of Events and Information	Remarks and references to Appendices
TEMPLEUX QUARRIES L.10.d.	1st		In Brigade support. Enemy attitude uncertain. Battle positions taken up at Stand-to morning and evening. Much shell gas used. no casualties. Nothing unusual to report. (2nd Lieut.) Girrulls (39/FE) appointed 2nd in Command and wears badges of rank of Major. Lt Soroney wounded. I.O.C. Shell-Shock.	236.
"	2nd			
"	3rd		Usual working-parties. Area much quieter than previous days. Military medals awarded to 3562 Sjt. E. McCarthy, No 253 Sjt. E. Buckett, No 3510 Cpl J. Homan No 10140 Pte J. Hough No 2353 Pte W. Brummell (see circular 6J 56/3 Intelligence of the 30.11.17) No casualties to day.	
"	4th		Officials. Lieut Doyle (PK) + Lts. E. J. Eastwood, E. O'Sullivan, C. O. Stiller, 99. Welsh. Asheries 7th Bn Northamptonshire in Batt. Minnow Sector. Usual patrols. hostile shelling on communication trenches more frequent. Enemy attitude more aggressive.	
HARGICOURT	5th		Front line more shelling than usual on front line. movements in BELLICOURT sector more pronounced. 2 M. wounded. Hisgow (Signaller) Lt O. B. Cullinan appointed Captain & Adjutant.	

WAR DIARY or INTELLIGENCE SUMMARY

Army Form C. 2118

December

Place	Date	Hour	Summary of Events and Information	Remarks and references to Appendices
HEBUTERNE	6th		Notification from No.3 C.C.S. – Capt. U. Ryves died of wounds 30 inst. A finer day. Enemy's attitude by day very quiet but rifle & rifle grenade at night - by any change of weather etc. Hostile front line apparently thinly probably 2 men at intervals of 100yds. Usual bursts of M.G. fire – no counter fire. Band on KIDLING and MOATRENT carried out two morning fire at Ashby and 15.OR. No identification obtained owing to enemy running back and Scutcombe Valley and to the grazed hits (fellowing) burst back so no trail of resistance. Casualties 1 P.E.(?)(attached) 3 O.R wounded (all killed).	
"	7th		A fine day. Usual patrols. Enemy holding front line very thinly. Increased activity in aerial work. Two aircraft down in BUCUCOURT (?) behind normal by Brit Aces. Enemy using the new Blue Cross Gas Shell and similar tears all behind our front line a days when the wind is to the west HM. a S.W. G.O.C. Brigade wounded. Lt. A. Bunder from Hospital.	
"	8th		A fine clear day. Sudden change from frost to warm has made approaches to front line almost impassable. PUCHEWAY S/I asst in water. Enemy's trenches equally bad, especially round CUBY and RUBY and he does appear to be moving. My as many of he enemy are seen to others and trenches frequently. – No casualties.	

WAR DIARY
or
INTELLIGENCE SUMMARY.

Army Form C. 2118.

December

Place	Date	Hour	Summary of Events and Information	Remarks and references to Appendices
HARGICOURT	10th		Lt Stafford. Langan to Asquit Corps. 2L brothers. Lt Spencer arrived also y other ranks. Reported by 9th Northamptonshires and go into Divisional Reserve at HERVILLY.	
HERVILLY	11th		Reinforcements Lt Spencer, Lt Surtees and y other ranks. Day devoted to cleaning and kit inspections. No working parties.	
"	12th		Refresher Courses started for junior NCOs and L. R.S.M. Smyth. M.C. Intensive training for boys. Lt Woods from hospital. Dr Girella to Hospital. Dr Gunter arrives.	
"	13th		Capt. P.B. Cullinan on leave to U.K. Inspection of Shin Loves by Divisional S.O.R. Lt U.R. on Boar. Many men found got. Y shin wounds. R.T.O.	
"	14th		Cipl Jones Major [?] R.D.F. Football won 3-1, 3 Jan been Lorry from Lois a Duris [?]	

WAR DIARY
INTELLIGENCE SUMMARY

Army Form C. 2118.

Place	Date	Hour	Summary of Events and Information	Remarks and references to Appendices
HÉBUTERNE	15th		O.R. to U.K.	
"	16th		a.m. Bn. threw to Regimental 9th Worcesters. Relief 17th Worcesters. m. BAIT-MIRROR seen.	
"	17th		Enemy much quieter. Snow flurries. patrols &c.	
"	18th		Heavy shelling around Bn. H.Q. and the front of Junction Emanation. "C" Coy + O.R. to U.K. Snow interferes patrols important.	
"	19th		Quiet day. Relieved by 12th Rifle Brigade.	
TEMPLEUX	20th		TEMPLEUX QUARRIES.	
"	21st		Relieved by L/Cpl Smith on leave to U.K. March to MONTIGNY.	
MONTIGNY	22nd		Coy. training. Arrivals Lts. Inspection by C.O. Lts. Fitzgerald & Taylor, and	
"	23rd		3 plenty. Departures 13. O.R. to U.K.	
"	24th		All Coys on Range 3 " " " Xmas Day celebrations. Church parade. Sports with	
"	25th		Americans. War horsing + tug o' war.	

DECEMBER 1914.

Army Form C. 2118.

WAR DIARY
or
INTELLIGENCE SUMMARY.

(Erase heading not required.)

Place	Date	Hour	Summary of Events and Information	Remarks and references to Appendices
MONTIGNY	26th		Lecture by Major Carroll 8th Buffs on organisation of coys.	
"	27th		Reconnaissance of POND sector. Guard mounting competition. B.Y.C. congratulates on re. smartness of turnout. Prize awarded to "C" Coy for general excellence.	
LEICESTER LOUNGE	28th		Relieved 8th Buffs in POND sector. Shelling rather heavy. no casualties.	
"	29th		Quiet day in tr. Reinforcements Lt Thornley and 37 O.R. arr'd.	
"	30th		Col. R. Bateman awarded M.M.	
"	31st		Quiet day.	

Army Form 2118.

WAR DIARY
INTELLIGENCE SUMMARY.
(Erase heading not required.)

Instructions regarding War Diaries and Intelligence Summaries are contained in F. S. Regs., Part II. and the Staff Manual respectively. Title pages will be prepared in manuscript.

WO 42

Place	Date	Hour	Summary of Events and Information	Remarks and references to Appendices
Ravenwood			2nd Battalion Leinster Regiment for the month of January 1918	

Army Form C. 2118.

January 1918

WAR DIARY
or
INTELLIGENCE SUMMARY.
(Erase heading not required.)

Instructions regarding War Diaries and Intelligence Summaries are contained in F. S. Regs., Part II. and the Staff Manual respectively. Title pages will be prepared in manuscript.

Place	Date	Hour	Summary of Events and Information	Remarks and references to Appendices
Lancashire Support	1.1.18		2nd Sector. Very quiet day. Intense cold and small snowstorms. 1. O.R. wounded.	T.S.C.
"	2.1.18		" Heavy snowfall. Daring patrol by 2/Lt Farrelly in front of POND TRENCH, entered enemy's line with Cpl Leah's. When coming round a corner he saw a sentry post. This post vacated their position in great alarm. 2/Lt Farrelly then poked Cpl Leah as sentry and entered a dug out above which he found unoccupied, but leaving evidence of recent occupation. Leaving Cpl Leah as sentry over this dug-out 2/Lt Farrelly came back to our own line and brought back a party to the enemy dug out where much valuable booty was obtained. For this action 2/Lt Farrelly was awarded the M.C. and Cpl Leah the 2nd bar to his M.M.	T.S.C.
"	3.1.18		2nd Sector. No shelling. Hard frost during night. Ground hard and as movement is easy everyone is cheerful. Good weather	

Army Form C. 2118.

WAR DIARY
or
INTELLIGENCE SUMMARY.
(Erase heading not required.)

January 1918

Place	Date	Hour	Summary of Events and Information	Remarks and references to Appendices
Leuckser Loupe	3.1.18		Frost sets quickly and rations are extremely good. Enemy's attitude just now rather difficult to understand as day & night patrols in No Mans Land have done their work unmolested. Ruby Wood farmer very silent. Major F.F. Fisman reported off Snior officers Course at AD & shot and assumes duties as 2nd in Command vice Greville to AD & shot on same Course	H.C.
"	4.1.18		Capt. J.T. Bullman reports off leave. Lt. Woods assumed N.C. Enemy aircraft over our lines to-day at 10 a.m. driven back by our fire. Our aircraft very active — several fights taking place well behind enemy's lines. Perhaps stopped with trains have been used extensively during this four for rations to stand or and have helped to reduce trench foot cases considerably. Lt. E.H.B. hopes to inspire	H.C.
"	5.1.18		9o Royal West Kents in daylight. W3 move to VENDELLES to Divisional Support. Reply over at 1.45 p.m.	

WAR DIARY or INTELLIGENCE SUMMARY

Army Form C. 2118.

Place	Date	Hour	Summary of Events and Information	Remarks and references to Appendices
VENDELLES	6-11-18		In Divisional Support. Large working party for improving 2nd line. Day spent in reconnoitring and selecting Battle positions in case of an enemy attack to seize high ground near COLOGNE FARM. Accommodation for men and officers very good.	
"	7-11-18		Helpful L/C. Reid awarded D.S.O. in recent Honours List. Capt Squires awarded M.C. Large working parties. Rain during night and had frost makes ground hazardly difficult to either ride or walk on.	
"	8-11-18		Usual working parties. 2nd Lt Thomas joins Bn. from 7th Leinsters. Appointed Artillery & Scout officer.	
"	9-11-18		Move to HANCOURT to Divisional Reserve, and take over billets occupied by 3rd Rifle Brigade who move to VENDELLES.	
HANCOURT	10-11-18		Day devoted to cleaning. No working parties. Intensive training started.	
"	11-11-18		Army Organised matches arranged with other units in Brigade. Hockey, Soccer and Rugby. Teams Capt. Vernon found.	

WAR DIARY or INTELLIGENCE SUMMARY

Army Form C. 2118.

January 1918

Place	Date	Hour	Summary of Events and Information	Remarks and references to Appendices
HAVRINCOURT	12.1.18		Intensive training. Snow during night making ground unpleasant. Lt Col. H.W. Weldon arrived and takes command of Batt. Major Friend 2/c in command. Major Freeman O.P.O.	
"	13.1.18		Church Parades. Lt Mathias & Lt Forbes joined from Hopoutre 4th Bayswell & Tommy. 4/30 Regt.	O.B.C.
"	14.1.18		Battalion working party. Concert for Bn Y.M.C.A. Capt Hall to Division as temporary A.A.C. to attachd General. R.O.N.S. Band Hymn Booking cancelled. Supplies taken employed in erecting temp. barricades around all huts.	
"	15.1.18		Working parties. The Brigade to run in Corps Reserve and work to bring line on the Corps line.	O.B.C.
"	16.1.18		Battalion working parties. All surplus labour employed on HAVRINCOURT defences.	
"	17.1.18		Battalion working parties on trps line R.P.C. quarter. Reconnoissance scheme at TINCOURT.	
"	18.1.18			
"	19.1.18		Battalion practising party. Info. Watching parts with 4/(5) Battalion at TINCOURT. Lt Col. H. Weldon taked Coptr. Hall or Secnd to R.F.	

Army Form C. 2118.

WAR DIARY
or
INTELLIGENCE SUMMARY.
(Erase heading not required.)

January 1916

Instructions regarding War Diaries and Intelligence Summaries are contained in F.S. Regs., Part II. and the Staff Manual respectively. Title pages will be prepared in manuscript.

Place	Date	Hour	Summary of Events and Information	Remarks and references to Appendices
HAMICOURT	20.1.18		Battalion working parties. Church parade at HAMICOURT.	
"	21.1.18		Battalion moved by Light Railway to KAISER trench to line POND SECTOR relieving 7th Buffs. Relief carried out without any casualties. Enemy's attitude rather more alert and vigorous than usual. "D" Coy in line "A" in support	
POND SECTOR	22.1.18		Very quiet day. Two men of "B" Company slightly wounded by our own working parties on INDANTRENCH.	
POND SECTOR	23.1.18		A number of aerial darts fired on POND TRENCH and SUPPORT. No casualties in front Coys though our artillery Signallers were killed by an aerial dart. The trenches are in a very bad condition. Two posts isolated during day time. Rations good and men main exceptionally good. The Company relief two men working in Indian Ounds struck an old German Bomb which exploded killing one and wounding the other. "B" Coy in line "B" in support.	
-do-	24.1.18		Very quiet day. Heavy fog. A few aerial darts on line but no casualties.	
-do-	25.1.18		Enemy very quiet. Buried his own men during into company relief. "B" Coy in line "C" in support.	
-do-	26.1.18		POND SECTOR. Enemy very active with aerial darts. Cpl Downey killed on a Coy Bridge	

WAR DIARY
or
INTELLIGENCE SUMMARY.
(Erase heading not required.)

Army Form C. 2118.

Place	Date	Hour	Summary of Events and Information	Remarks and references to Appendices
Lagnicourt Lounge	28.1.18 (contd)		wounded by our own shell which fell in the front line. Trenches in an extremely bad condition. Rations & rum good.	
	27.1.18		Relief Company relief. 'B' in front line, 'D' in Support. Cpl. Leslie M.M. (the two) wounded by sniper. Cpl Dwosey buried in HARICOURT Cemetery. Enemy fairly quiet. A Contour'd artillery, machine gun & sniping shots arranged by Major Ford D.S.O. at 12 mnyts to commemorate the form of the Kaisers birthday, was very successfully carried out.	
	28.1.18		Very foggy day. Enemy very quiet but 'C' Company very aggressive. Large enemy working party thought near Riencourt was by Lewis Gun & rifle fire. Relief Company Relief. 'D' Coy in front line, 'C' in Support. Enemy very quiet but alert. No casualties. Wiring working party in Sudan Sunset. Stay Sunny.	
	29.1.18		new Lincoln Lounge heavily shelled by 15cm guns. No damage caused and quite a lot of ammunition wasted by Kultur. Fwd. Sectn. Enemy shelled Harguncline lightly at 4 pm. Our artillery retaliates on Malakoff Wood. The Battalion was relieved by the Norfolks and returns	
	30.1.18		to Martigny Farm in Brigade Support.	

WAR DIARY
or
INTELLIGENCE SUMMARY.
(Erase heading not required.)

Army Form C. 2118.

Place	Date	Hour	Summary of Events and Information	Remarks and references to Appendices
Antwerp	31.1.19		Inter battalion sports with Royal Sussex Regt. Hockey. Inspg of regt. left arm by battalion. The battalion received orders to move to Incourt on the 9th Feb. to form the 16th Division. All ranks very sorry to have any connection with the 2nd Division. During the time with the Division the battalion has the following Casualties 100 officers 1862 OR. Honours gained VC's 1 DSO's 5 MC's 15 Bars to MC 1. DCM's 8 MM's 60 Bars to MM 3. Second bars to MM 1. MSM 1. Belgian Croix de guerre 2.	

Signed
Lieut Colonel
Comdg. 2nd Bn The Queen's Regt

www.ingramcontent.com/pod-product-compliance
Lightning Source LLC
Chambersburg PA
CBHW080912230426
43667CB00015B/2660